EMPIRES COME, EMPIRES GO

SIDNEY OWITZ

authorHOUSE®

AuthorHouse™
1663 Liberty Drive
Bloomington, IN 47403
www.authorhouse.com
Phone: 833-262-8899

Published by AuthorHouse 01/21/2021

ISBN: 978-1-6655-1433-0 (sc)
ISBN: 978-1-6655-1432-3 (e)

Print information available on the last page.

This book is printed on acid-free paper.

DEDICATION

This book is dedicated to my wife, Joan, and our children, Stephanie, Valerie, David, Darron, Carole, Jeff and Robin

Go as far as you can see; when you get there, you will be able to see further.

Thomas Carlyle (1795-1881).

CONTENTS

THE RAPE OF EUROPE

———◆◇◆———

IN GREEK MYTHOLOGY EUROPA WAS the daughter of Phoenix. She was a most beautiful woman, a Phoenician princess. One day she was abducted by Zeus who swam with her to Crete where he seduced her or raped her (apparently both words have the same meaning in ancient Greek). One of her sons was Minos, the King of Crete. The continent of Europe is named after Europa, as was one of the moons of Jupiter. Like Europa the continent of Europe has also been raped or invaded – not once, but innumerable times throughout its history. Europe is the birthplace of Western civilization, and also the graveyard of its people who succumbed to dictators, tyrants and mobsters from within and without, people who dared to destroy any peace on the continent. However, in order to preserve the inhabitants of Europe and something as great as it's civilization it had to be fought for because if there was no fight there would have been no civilization. Out of Europe came the inventors whose minds opened up a better world for us to live in, and brave men who conquered the High Seas and the hidden lands of the unexplored continents.

What about the revolutions fought not against governments, but for the advancement of knowledge as in the Age of Enlightenment and for the invention of better machines to replace manual labor as in the Industrial Revolution? All this culminated in Modern Civilization and two World Wars, supposedly to end all wars. It did not accomplish that goal, but it made wars even more dangerous and fearful by introducing nuclear warfare and other dangerous weapons. The Second World War created an atmosphere of distrust, not only amongst the combatants, but also among the victors. It introduced the Cold War between the USSR and the West. After the World Wars, Europe lost its dominance, which was then taken over and shared by the United States and the Soviet Union.

Today the nations of Europe are united in a European Union which was meant to bind the nations as one and to bring peace to Europe after millennia of wars.

PERSIA

The first formidable empire was the Persian Empire which was founded by Cyrus. He conquered Babylon in 539 B.C. Babylon had been somewhat of an empire on its own right. Nebuchadnezzar of Babylon had conquered Judah and laid waste to Jerusalem, destroying the Temple and sending the Jews into exile in Babylon. In those days defeating a nation frequently led to exile of its people to the conqueror's land where they could learn the new language and get to know the habits and rituals of the host nation while the conqueror would send some of his own people to the conquered territory in order to re-build, set up their own monuments and take over the government.

When Cyrus the Great of Persia conquered Babylon he allowed the Jews, who had been exiled to Babylon to return to the Holy Land if they so wished, and gave them permission to re-build their Temple. Jews praised Cyrus for his sympathy and understanding.

The Persian Empire extended from Mesopotamia to India and from the Nile to the Balkans, the Black Sea and Central Asia. We call the land Persia because the original tribal name of the country was Parsua. Their language Farsi is derived from the same name. The capital was Persepolis. The Persians introduced standard currency and a system of weights and measures into their dominions. They spread the Aramaic language to their lands of conquest, as well as the arts of metal work and carpet weaving. They increased commerce and trade on three continents, and they built roads and canals. They set up small areas of administration under - what they called – satraps in order to help in ruling this over-sized Empire. Although they were Zoroastrians by religion, they did not force Zoroastrianism on their conquered people.

The Persians invaded Greece because the Greeks had supported the Ionian cities in their revolt against the Persians. This caused Darius I to be very annoyed, so he invaded Greece, but was defeated by the Spartans at Marathon. Xerxes (known as Ahasuerus in the Book of Esther), who followed his father Darius I, wanted revenge for his father's defeat, so with a very large army he invaded Greece. He crossed the Hellespont in 480 B.C. and defeated the Spartans at Thermopylae, He moved into Athens and sacked the city. It was not until 333 B.C. that Alexander the Great defeated the Persians under Darius III and drove them out of Greece. This created a depletion of the finances of the Persian Empire, and weakened the mighty giant among nations. From then on, the Persian Empire went downhill and came to an end after about 200 years of dominating the known world.

GREEK AND ROMAN EMPIRES

Invasions did not always come from the outside of Europe. They sometimes came from within and spread their conquering forces as far and as wide as they could. Take for example the Greek civilization which was supposed to have commenced in about 1200 B.C. Their empire continued until the Romans defeated them at the Battle of Corinth in 146 B.C. Was there a Greek Empire? Actually Philip II was King of Macedonia, which was not a part of Greece; it was a separate land to the north of Greece. Philip invaded Greece in 336 B.C., making Greece a part of his territory. It was his son, Alexander the Great, who continued with the invasions that his father had started. We would never have heard of Alexander if his father had not developed the army and had not had the foresight to attack a weakened and turbulent Greece. Alexander went to war against the Persians and defeated Darius. Then he went about spreading the Empire even further by conquering all the lands between Egypt and India. So why do we not call it the Macedonian Empire? Both Philip and Alexander the Great were Macedonians and had nothing to do with Greece until they conquered it and the rest of the surrounding territories. The reason is that Macedonia had made no contribution to Western civilization, but it was the Greek culture that survived throughout the Macedonian occupation and spread throughout the civilized world affecting the lives of the conquered nations, as it affects our lives even until this day. Thanks to Philip and his son, Alexander, who died at the age of 32 and preserved

Greek culture for humanity. Roman, Christian and Western civilization have benefited from and built on Greek philosophy, literature, science, art, sculpture and development of the human body.

When the Greek Empire reached the Holy Land the Jews respected the Greeks. They were somewhat embarrassed by the nudity displayed by them during exercise, but they appreciated their culture and teachings. They had a good relationship with Alexander the Great who occupied their country but did not destroy their Temple as Nebuchadnezzar had done before him. The Samaritans complained to Alexander about the Jews, but he told the Jews that he would turn a blind eye on their handling of their Samaritan problems. The Jews did not think in the same way as the Greeks. The Jews considered Holy to be beautiful; the Greeks considered beautiful to be Holy.

After the death of Alexander there was a great deal of fighting between the surviving hierarchy. The problem was finally solved by dividing the Empire into four sections – the Ptolemaic section which ruled Egypt and its environs, the Seleucid portion covering Mesopotamia, a section for Central Asia and the Attalid leadership which controlled Asia Minor including Anatolia.

The Greek Empire continued to rule much of the civilized world until the Romans developed their own civilization and later defeated them in the Macedonian Wars. It was not until the final battle at Corinth in 146 B.C. that the Romans were in command. The Romans copied the Greeks in art, architecture and religion. Once the Roman Empire grew it was found that Greek was the most spoken language in the Empire while Athens, not Rome, remained the center of learning. The Romans propagated the Greek culture and Hellenism. It was Greek culture that was the force that carried the Roman Empire. Jews were prominent within the Empire, claiming to be God's Chosen People, but Hellenism would not accept that God would choose one group of people over another. They also could not understand why the Jews would not respect them by worshipping the Greek gods as well as their own.

Romaniotes were Jews who came to the Roman Empire from Jerusalem after the sacking of the second Temple by the Romans in about 72 A.D., adding to the Jewish population who had already been living there. Some had arrived in Greece from the time of Alexander the Great.

The Romaniotes spoke a Judeo-Greek language mixed with Aramaic. They still exist in Israel and New York, and are the oldest Jewish group in the world, having been through the Holocaust after Hitler over-ran Greece in the Second World War. They had been living in Greece ever since the days of the Greek Empire. The Romaniotes received their name from the Byzantine Empire which at that time was known as Rhomania in eastern Europe.

Paul at this time had been traveling around Crete and Greece, promoting Christianity. The Gospels were first written in Greek. The first church in Rome was a Greek church. Only when Rome burnt in 64 A.D. did Nero blame the Christians and started persecuting them. It was said that Nero used the burning of Rome as a political agenda. He then re-built Rome in his own way. Christianity was not welcome in Rome after that – even the Jews were better tolerated than the Christians at that time and until the early fourth century. Christians who did not worship the Roman gods were sometimes thrown to the beasts. Not until 312 A.D. did Constantine convert to Christianity, and thereafter he made it the religion of the Roman Empire.

Why did the mighty Roman Empire fall? There are probably many reasons for this, some more important than others. Basically, it was because of the barbarians. They had been hammering at the gates of the Roman Empire for at least a century, but the Romans did not allow them to enter. Gradually, as Rome grew weaker, the Goths started to cross the border. The Romans were running short of slaves as a result of a cessation in expansion of their territories so they reluctantly allowed the Goths to enter and made them fill the role of the dwindling slaves. They were oppressed as slaves until they finally revolted. They were successful in their revolt because many of them had been brought into the Roman legions initially where they had received military training before they turned them into slaves. In fact, these inadvertent instructions which they had received while they were serving in the Roman army enabled Alaric and his men to sack Rome. The Barbarians set up their own territories within the Roman Empire. When the Barbarians displayed their strength the Roman weakness became more obvious and Germanic tribes like the Vandals and Saxons stormed into the Empire while some moved into Gaul and as far as Britain (all Roman territories).

It has been said that the advent of Christianity helped to weaken Rome. Before Constantine the Emperor had always been held in high esteem by the subjects, almost like a deity. When Constantine introduced Christianity to the Empire in the first half of the 4th century making it the sole religion of the Roman Empire, the Pope and the Church suddenly became adored and more powerful causing the Emperor to lose status as a god while Jesus received the love and prayers of the people. With a standstill in expansion, a faltering economy and fewer slaves to do the hard labor the infrastructure, which was sorely in need of repair was fast deteriorating. The aqueduct system was causing bad hygiene, sewage was present in the streets, and scavenging animals were running around loosely and out of control. Infectious diseases, malaria and plague were taking their toll. At the same time there was government corruption and political instability.

Even before Constantine there was Diocletian from Croatia who ruled as Emperor. In 284 Diocletian recognized all the problems of the Roman Empire, and he decided to divide and rule. He split the Empire into the Western Roman Empire with its capital in Rome and the eastern Byzantine Empire with its capital in Constantinople. The two Empires were ruled by a tetrarchy, which means rule by four emperors – two for each Empire, one emperor and a second-in-command who would take over if and when needed. Diocletian ruled over the eastern part since he was from that region and was not too enamored with Rome. The Western Roman Empire came to its end towards the end of the fifth century whereas the eastern Byzantine Empire continued for almost another thousand years until it was taken over by the Ottomans in 1452 at the siege of Constantinople. At first the division of the Empire had seemed like a good idea, but as the Byzantine Empire expanded the Roman Empire continued to fail. Constantinople was fortified and became almost invincible. Rome was not protected, hence the sacking by Alaric. Yet despite the fall of the Roman Empire its influence in the arts and culture built upon the Greek culture which it had inherited, have continued even until this day.

HOLY ROMAN EMPIRE

A few hundred years after the demise of the Roman Empire we see the beginnings of a new Empire wherein the people displayed nostalgia for the past – the old Roman Empire. On Christmas Day 800 A.D. Pope Leo III crowned Charlemagne Emperor of the defunct Roman Empire. Both the Pope and people in leadership positions wanted to retain the name of the Roman Empire for its prestige, even though it had disappeared over three hundred years before. At this stage it was mostly a German Kingdom, but included areas of Northern Italy and some of Bohemia, and later Burgundy was added. The Pope crowned Charlemagne because he wanted the Church to be stronger than the Emperor whereas Charlemagne wished to be in charge of the holy regions. In the 10th century Otto I, grandson of Charlemagne, was crowned by Pope John XII. It was then that the name of Holy was added to Roman Empire, stressing the relationship to the Catholic Church. In the 12th century Frederick Barbarossa (meaning red beard) accentuated his imperial desire to dominate Italy and the Catholic Church. He did not wish to take second place behind the Pope. He marched into Italy and occupied most of Northern Italy. He was considered to be one of the strongest of the Holy Roman Empire's leaders. Voltaire, at the end of the eighteenth century commented that the Holy Roman Empire was neither Holy, nor Roman, nor an Empire. It was a mis-named entity, yet it lasted until 1806 (one thousand years) when Napoleon invaded the territory and named it the Confederation of the Rhine.

During the existence of the Holy Roman Empire there was no capital. Wherever the Emperor lived or whichever city he desired became his capital. There were numerous smaller monarchies within the Empire where kings and other types of leaders reigned, but they were all subservient to the Emperor. The Holy Roman Empire never achieved political unification, but always consisted of decentralized self-governing units.

The Holy Roman Empire was frequently involved in squabbles and wars with other states in Europe, but the biggest and most important of these confrontations was the Thirty Years War which lasted from 1618 to 1648. It was a war between Germany (ruled by the Habsburgs) and France. Over 8 million people were killed in the war or died from disease during that period. It started as a religious war. Ferdinand II of the Holy Roman

Empire wanted all the people in his land to be Catholic. The Protestants in the Empire revolted against such an extreme demand. The war spread into many countries in Europe with Denmark, Sweden, Bohemia and Spain joining in. Spain invaded France and occupied it for some time. Catholic France actually fought on the side of the Protestants because of her hatred for the Habsburgs. The Treaty of Westphalia ended the war whereby the power of the Catholics was diminished and Spain lost control of Portugal and the Low Countries.

Interestingly, the Habsburg family that ruled the Holy Roman Empire for over many centuries and only ended their rule when Napoleon defeated them in 1806, were anti-Nazi when Hitler took over the German Reich in 1933. They were persecuted by Hitler. The USSR did not like them either during the Cold War as they feared their adverse effect upon East Germany and the Soviet satellite states.

THE VIKINGS

The Vikings came from Scandinavia – Denmark, Sweden and Norway. They were considered to be violent heathens and savages, with no education. They traded with and raided the countries around them, as far afield as Iceland, the Northern British Isles, the Faroe Islands, Finland, Newfoundland and Greenland. They frequently lived near the coast-line and had easy access to the seas, thus becoming great sailors and builders of long boats. Their craftsmanship of long boats and their navigational skills, coupled with their boldness, enabled them to sail away from their domestic seas and venture into foreign waters where they continued with their raiding, trading and piracy. They settled in the northern British Isles including Ireland and the Orkneys. Their ships entered the Mediterranean where they plied their trade. They arrived in Turkey long before the Ottoman Empire was formed and at the same time were present in Baghdad. They went to North-East Europe, Belarus and the Ukraine. They explored Europe through their seas and rivers. They sailed down the Volga. When they were in European Russia they were known as the Rus. 'Rus' translates as 'the men who row' in Old Norse terms. If they liked what they saw around them they would just settle, no matter where it was. They went to live in the Ukraine where they were known as the Kievian Rus.

The height of their activity occurred between the eighth century and 1066. They absorbed the culture of the lands that they occupied and at the same time their Norse culture was imprinted upon the Europeans. In the Norse language the word Vik means a crack or an inlet or small bay. This may be the origin of their name as Norway is a country of fjords and that is where they mastered their art of seamanship.

What motivated the Vikings to seek other lands? Women are an important part of the answer. In Scandinavia each male of the higher classes had a number of wives, leaving an insufficient number of women for most of the men who were not of the higher classes. They sought out women on their voyages to bring home as wives. The best women they took for themselves, while the rest of their captives became their slaves. There were three classes in society - thralls who were the slaves, the Karls who were middle class and the Jarls who were distinctly upper class and possessed most of the wives.

The Vikings were in Britain from 860, and many of the British people today are offspring from those original Vikings who settled there. Many words in the English language have their derivation from the Vikings, including the days of the week which honor the Norse gods. They raided the north of England and the Isle of Man, and they settled there, making York as their capital in England. In fact, the North of England belonged to the Vikings. They called it Danelaw. They were in London, but King Alfred took London from them, and he ruled in the south of England even though Vikings were also living in the south of England under him. Angles, Saxons and Jutes, who were originally Scandinavians, too, had arrived in England after settling in Germany.

When Harold became King of the southern part of England he went north and routed the Vikings of Danelaw, driving them out of England. However, while he was involved in the north William the Conqueror and the Normans crossed over from Normandy in 1066. Harold had to rush down from the north to defend his land against William. It was too much for him, and his forces were defeated. Strange to say, but William the Conqueror, too, was a Viking. His ancestors had been Vikings who had come to settle in Normandy some time before that. On the arrival of the

Normans (or Norsemen) in Northern France in about 1000 the authorities, in order to prevent further looting and rioting, gave them a tract of land in Normandy so that they could live peacefully as good citizens. They did so and became Christians.

The Vikings were in Ireland from 795 to 1014. For a certain period of time they ruled Ireland. They created Waterford, the first city in Ireland – also, Dublin and Cork. They introduced trade between Ireland, England and Scandinavia, and later with Europe. These trade routes became well established. The production of money was developed at the same time. In 1014 Brian Baru drove the Viking leadership out of Ireland, but there is much Viking DNA in the Irish population. Many words in the Irish language are of Viking origin.

When the Vikings arrived in Europe there was a weakness of leadership in most areas. The Western part of the Roman Empire had fallen in the fifth century. The seventh century saw the surge of Islam into Spain. Everything was in turmoil. The Vikings were able to settle in to European countries fairly easily without too much fighting. Charlemagne of the Holy Roman Empire encouraged them to accept Christianity – he actually gave them a choice of baptism or death - which in turn helped to put an end to their raiding, piracy and violence, transforming them into model citizens. The Vikings in central Europe became Christians long before their Scandinavian homelands adopted Christianity which was as late as the 11th century.

MONGOL EMPIRE

I was recently given a gift in the form of an invitation to have my ancestry explored by a well-known organization. I spat into a small bottle and sent the specimen to the organization. As expected, they found that I was an Ashkenazi Jew – but they also found a small percentage of Mongolian DNA in my chromosomes. How is that possible? I asked myself. I am sure that in those days of diminished mobility my ancestors could never have made that dangerous trip, as Marco Polo had done, along the Silk Road, through the Gobi Desert and much of Asia to Mongolia, and then back again to Europe. It must be wrong; my ancestors were never adventurers or explorers. We know that the Mongol Empire spread into eastern Europe. Who are these Mongols who vilified and defiled my ancestral grandmother? I immediately decided to investigate this phenomenon, and to take action if necessary, in order to retrieve my family honor! I would not rest until I discovered who placed that small percentage of Mongolian DNA into my ancestral chromosomes.

Mongolia has been an isolated land in Asia for thousands of years, with no outlet to the sea and hemmed in by larger and far more powerful countries along its borders, including China to the south and Russia to the north. It is a land-locked country with hot summers and very cold and icy winters. The Gobi Desert occupies the southern portion of the country. Those who are not of Mongolian descent are likely to be Kazakhs, a western neighbor with a similar life-style. The people of Mongolia, about three million of them, are predominantly semi-nomadic as most of the land is grassland and not arable. Buddhism is the predominant religion while the rest of the people have no religion, relying mostly in shamanism. Inhabitants are known for their falconry and horsemanship. None of these characteristics have shown up in my ancestry – nor in me!

Out of this inhospitable wilderness was born Genghis Khan, who became the founder of the largest Empire the world until that time had ever known. Only the British Empire, nine hundred years later, was larger in size than the Mongol Empire at its height.

Genghis Khan was born in 1162. He soon realized that he was surrounded by a world of violence. His father had kidnapped the woman who became his wife and bore Genghis. His father died from poisoning by an enemy. Genghis Kahn killed his own brother. There were constant raids from neighboring tribes. Life was brutal. He realized that he had to be always alert in order to remain alive. Despite constant vigilance he was captured by another tribe while still a young man. He remained as their prisoner, but finally escaped and proceeded to form his own military unit in order to seek vengeance on his captors. He soon overcame them, as well as surrounding tribes and became their leader, forcing them to join him in his own army. His strength grew and his army swept through the land, growing as he advanced, until he became the ruler of the entire Mongolian landscape. Then he set about conquering most of Asia.

He imposed rigid discipline amongst his forces. He was a military genius, and despite cruelty and the slaughtering of his foes he allowed religious freedom in all the countries that he occupied, even though he had no religion himself. He forbade torture among his people and stopped the trading of women for sex and slavery. He set up a diplomatic system among the countries in his domain. He encouraged trade amongst the subjects of his territory, and was the first to develop a postal system throughout his lands. He used horsemen to deliver the mail, and developed a relay system of horsemen which sometimes traveled over thousands of miles. His power and leadership were felt all over his Empire – and outside. The people of the conquered lands referred to the Mongol invaders as the Golden Horde. The strange and powerful Mongol leader who had most of Asia under his control fell off his horse one day. He never recovered from that fall, yet he continued to lead his army until he died in 1227.

He was followed by his son, Ogedei, who continued in his father's footsteps. Ogedei was a charismatic character, and was able to hold on to the lands conquered by his father. In fact, his cavalry continued south and west, absorbing south Asia and Persia into his Empire. He did not stop there, but crossed over into Europe, taking in his stride Russia, Poland, Hungary and Bulgaria. It must have been in Poland or Lithuania where one of his cavalrymen confronted my ancestral grandmother whose parents and grandparents had come across Europe searching for a peaceful land where they could live without fear of having to fight anti-Semitism and persecution. When the wandering Jews finally reached Poland, all had appeared to be calm and hospitable until Ogedai arrived.

Ogedei's aim appears to have been to reach the Atlantic, but his plans were thwarted by his death, probably as a result of alcoholism. Guyuk was the son of Ogedei and the third Khan of the Mongol Empire. He came into conflict with the Pope even while he continued to rein in more of Europe into his realm. He only ruled for two years, and his life ended in the way of many of Genghis Kahn's offspring, which was from the complications of alcoholism – even though Genghis Kahn did not suffer from this problem.

Kublai Khan, the grandson of Genghis Khan, became the leader of the Mongol Empire in 1260 and ruled until 1294. As a child he showed a great interest in the Chinese portion of the Empire. The first few years after taking control of the Empire he fought many battles against his brother and his followers, but finally defeated them at Xanadu. "In Xanadu did

Kublai Khan a stately pleasure dome decree" according to Samuel Taylor Coleridge. He continued gaining more land within Chinese territory, and even moved his capital from Karakorum, which was badly destroyed in his battles with his brother, to China, apparently where Beijing stands today. After defeating the rulers of China, the Song Dynasty, he founded the Yuan Dynasty. At this stage the Mongol Empire stretched from the Pacific through Siberia, the Indian sub-continent and Afghanistan to the Black Sea and into Europe. The Mongol Empire between 1270 and 1309 was the largest contiguous land mass ruled by man in the history of the world even unto this day. It had a landmass of 9.15 million square miles. It was 16% of the world's land mass and contained 25% of the entire world population. The British Empire was larger in square miles, but it was not contiguous. Its lands were far-flung across the oceans throughout the world.

Kublai Khan was really only interested in China and Mongolia – the rest of the Empire was left to others to control. His style of governing was not to impose his will upon the people, but to allow them to live much as they had lived in the past and only to encourage and aid them, as far as possible in their demands. He was criticized for being more interested in China than in Mongolia. The people asked what was to become of Mongolia while he was so busy with China? Nevertheless, he created ports and canals, he developed trade routes and formed alliances. He tried to increase the size of the Empire, but failed in his attempted invasions of Japan, Java and Vietnam.

The first sign of the cracking of the Empire came when Kublai Khan and his brother went to war with each other. There were further battles with other members of the family which seemed to become commonplace. The Mamluks of Egypt, who were originally Muslim slaves that had overtaken the Egyptian government and defeated the Crusaders, stopped Kublai Khan from spreading his Empire westward. By concentrating his attention on Mongolia and China only, Kublai Khan lost control of the other Asian and European sectors of his domain. The Plague or Black Death spread deeply into his territory, and added a strain on his resources. Finally, the Ming Dynasty in China overthrew his Yuan Dynasty in 1368, and the Mongolian Empire teetered until it was shattered. It is also said that the weather changes in Europe at that time caused a great deal of flooding which prevented the Mongol cavalrymen from moving forward in their usual massive hordes. Therefore, they were forced to turn southwards, inadvertently saving the rest of Europe. Strangely, the Moghuls (stemming from the Mongols) continued to rule India well into the nineteenth century when the British drove them out of the sub-continent in 1860.

We have here another massive Empire that could not hold on to its territory and faded into the annals of history almost never to be heard from again, except when I heard about the finding of Mongolian DNA in my blood-stream.

THE BLACK DEATH

We are discussing the effect of Empires on the European population. Obviously, the Black Death does not refer to an Empire, but the effect on the people was no less than a conquest by a dictator. The death toll and the effects on life are comparable, if not worse.

Between 1347 and 1351 Europe suffered a gigantic invasion which killed about 100 million people. This was not an invasion of armies of people but one of micro-organisms. The Black Death (or the Plague, as it is now known) was the result of this invasion. The pandemic started in Asia and traveled along the Silk Road to the west. Genoese sailors probably transported it to Constantinople, and from there it moved into Europe and Africa. It was caused by a bacterium called Yersinia pestis (Yersin was a student of Louis Pasteur). The organism was carried by the flea that picked it up from feeding on the blood and secretions of rats or from corpses of dead rats, and then passing it on to humans. Humans, bitten by the flea would find large swellings in their groins or arm-pits involving lymph nodes, known as bubos (hence the term Bubonic Plague). The infections resulting from these bites would be carried away to the draining lymph glands and then suppurate. People were less conscious of cleanliness in those days than they are today and there was no such thing as insecticide sprays, so the fleas and the germs were left to cause their damage freely. If the lungs became infected one would have Pneumonic Plague. There was also a form of Septicemic Plague when the bacteria would be carried in the blood-stream – the most fatal. The plague attacked Europe after a famine when many people were suffering from malnutrition and had low resistance with a poor immune response.

As in all wars and times of hardship there had to be a scapegoat. Jews and gypsies were blamed for the Black Death. The Jewish populations of Cologne, Strasbourg and numerous other European cities were decimated, not only by the Plague, but also from being killed by members of the general population because they were accused of having poisoned the wells even though they drank from the same wells as the general population and died at the same rate. These attacks upon the Jews were one reason for the Jewish migration to Poland where they were welcomed and warmly accepted. It took Europe many decades to make up for the severe population loss caused by the Black Death.

OTTOMAN EMPIRE

Throughout the fourteenth century a Turkic people living in Anatolia expanded their territory by raiding neighboring tribes. The area under their control kept growing, and by the time that Osman Gazi, a Turkman born in Anatolia in 1256, became their leader their territory had become well established and formidable. Osman gave his name to the people and the country. They were called the Ottomans or, as the Arabs referred to them, the Uttmans. Islam had already become a religious faith in Anatolia. It had already spread far into Africa, Asia and Europe. In 1453 Mehmed II, the Ottoman leader at that time, captured Constantinople, the capital of the Byzantine Empire, putting an end to the eastern section of the historic Roman Empire which had outlived its brother Empire, the Roman Empire, by a thousand years. The Ottomans ruled as a Caliphate, expanded into Europe, Asia, the Middle East, North Africa as far as the Horn of Africa, becoming the largest Empire in the world. At the end of World War I the Ottoman Empire was defeated, dismantled and partitioned by the Western Allies. Today, Turkey is the heir to the remnants of the mighty Ottoman Empire.

During its years of expansion the Ottoman Empire was Persianized by adopting much of the Persian language, their culture, literature and ways of life. Don't forget, both were Islamic by religion, even though the

Ottomans were Sunni and the Persians were Shia. Being at the cross-roads of the world, the Ottoman Empire held a strategic position. In 1521 Suleiman the Magnificent conquered Belgrade followed by an advance into Hungary. They moved into Transylvania and Moldovia. In 1593 they searched for a way of penetrating further into Europe, but they were held back at Vienna. In the 16th and 17th centuries the Ottomans controlled much of the Caucasus, sharing the real estate with the Persians. The Black Sea became an Ottoman lake, thus preventing the czars of Russia from having any access into the Mediterranean. The Ottoman navy was the most dominant force in the Mediterranean. When they turned their attention to the Middle East, Syria and Mesopotamia as far as the Persian Gulf it was not difficult for them to bring these territories under their influence. They next moved into Egypt and other areas of Arabic-speaking North Africa. All they needed was to desire a land, and it became theirs!

The Ottomans did not conquer Persia, because they could not. Even though they were both Muslim peoples they were serious rivals. Persia is a very mountainous land, difficult to invade. The population is relatively small for such a large land mass. If an invading army of Ottomans had arrived there would have been insufficient crops growing there to feed this large army. Therefore, the invaders would have had to drag supplies from the Mediterranean through the mountainous landscape of Persia. The Ottomans experienced a number of wars with the Persians and soon realized what a problem a real invasion would be to them, so they never attempted to do so.

Between 1740 and 1768 the Ottomans went through a period of peace, but during those years the Habsburgs and the Russians strengthened their military might becoming more of a match for them. However, the Ottoman Empire had become too vast; it spread in so many directions and it was too difficult to keep control over every province, especially as these were times of slow transportation. There was also a good deal of in-fighting within the administration during this era while many of the lands in their domain began to seek their independence. Signs of weakness were soon visible. The Ottoman Empire became known as the 'sick man of Europe'.

Between the 17th and 20th centuries the Russians and the Ottomans fought twelve wars. The Russians wanted to use some of her ports on the Black Sea, but the Ottomans had total control of the entire Black

Sea. In 1676 the Russians tried taking back the Crimean Peninsula, but failed. However, in 1774 the Russians were able to get back the Caucasus and finally reach the Black Sea. This war demonstrated to the world a weakening of the power of the Ottomans.

What is known as the Crimean War took place in 1856. Here the Ottomans defeated the Russians because the French and the British fought on their side. The British feared Russian expansion into the Eastern Mediterranean and Asia while the French fought because the Russians had pushed them out of the Holy Places in Jerusalem which was under control of the Ottoman Empire. Russia lost a half a million men due to the war and disease. The Russian economy was failing. They were humiliated, yet the Turks, too, underwent a decline in morale because, even though they were on the winning side, they realized that their weaponry was outdated as compared to their Allies and their enemies. On the other hand, the war brought more Western trade to Turkey which was introduced by her new Allies, Britain and France. This gave the Sultan encouragement to improve his grip on the Caliphate and attempt to turn the decline of the Empire around. The British and French were helping the Ottomans for the express purpose of holding the Russians in check.

In 1821 Greece fought for its independence from the Ottomans, and became the first independent state in the Empire. In 1875 Herzegovina revolted, and this spread to Bosnia and Bulgaria. The Turks massacred the revolutionaries. Russia went to the aid of the Serbs, who were also a Slavic people, initiating another Russo-Turkish war. Otto Von Bismarck, at the Congress of Berlin, helped to settle the Balkan problems. He gave Cyprus (an Ottoman possession) to Britain and allowed Austria to occupy Bosnia and Herzegovina while Russia took Georgia and Armenia, all of which further weakened the Ottomans. He did not seem to give too much to the Ottomans apart from allowing them to hold on to Macedonia, yet the Turks still liked Bismarck.

One of the reasons for the disintegration of the Ottoman Empire is probably the fact that they chose the wrong side at the beginning of World War I. They chose Germany who lost the war, and the Ottomans came tumbling down together with their Germans allies. Had they fought with the Entente Cordiale, who had come to their rescue during the Crimean War, they would probably have survived as an Empire.

THE BRITISH EMPIRE

In the 16th century Britain was not as great a naval power as the Spanish and Portuguese. When Spanish ships were coming back from a war in the Netherlands they planned to invade England. Phillip II of Spain wished to eradicate Protestantism, considered to be a foul religion and an enemy of the Catholic Church. The Spanish had also reported that Drake and his men had been pirating Spanish vessels in the Caribbean. Nevertheless, Sir Frances Drake defeated the Spanish Armada at Gravelines, off the British coast, in 1588, perhaps with the help of severe weather conditions that were supposed to have pushed the Spanish ships northward. These were the same British who had been assisting the Dutch during their fight for independence from Spain. Britain developed more confidence following her naval victory. She wished to emulate the examples set by the explorers of Spain and Portugal, and from that time set her sights upon procuring overseas colonies.

The first permanent settlement in the New World was in Jamestown, Virginia in 1607. This colony almost failed because the settlers had chosen an area in which to live that turned out to be a bad choice - a foul swampy area, with no fresh water. At first, they thought there were no Indians in the vicinity, but they soon met up with the Powhatan Indians with whom they had an on and off relationship. The Powhatan Indians became sick and were dying because of illnesses introduced to them by the settlers. Many of the colonists died, too, but they were replenished with more settlers from England. However, in 1676 the settlement was deliberately burnt down. In 1699 the settlers returned to Virginia and the colony was re-built. They introduced new people and fresh crops, and grew tobacco and sugar.

Britain commenced colonization in a number of North American locations. The original Jamestown settlement preceded the 1620 settlers of Pilgrims who were Calvinists seeking freedom from the Church of England whom they felt had wandered too far from their religion. The Pilgrims landed in Massachusetts. Later, they were followed by the Puritans. The Pilgrims were separatists from the Church of England whereas the Puritans were non-separatists (they wanted to remain within their Church, but wished to change it).

We can see that Britain firmly implanted herself into the North American continent and the Caribbean in the 17ᵗʰ century. In 1623 Britain occupied St. Kitts, and two years later they took Barbados. Nevus, Antigua and Montserrat followed in quick succession. In 1655 the British occupied Jamaica which was being held by a small Spanish force. British settlers proceeded to grow sugar and tobacco with the help of slaves. In 1664 New Amsterdam was taken from the Dutch, and that became New York. In 1681 New Sweden, which had been a Swedish and then a Dutch colony, was taken over at the arrival of William Penn, and that was divided between Pennsylvania and Delaware. Acadia, which consisted of parts of Quebec, the Maritime Provinces of Canada and the north of Maine, had been in British hands, but was returned to France in 1632. It was re-taken from the French in 1713. During the Seven Years War Britain drove the French out of much of Canada. Small wonder that France supported the American colonies in their war against the British when fighting for their independence!

The American War of Independence started because the colonists were becoming united and were unhappy with the Crown ruling from many thousands of miles away, imposing taxation without representation and forcing them to re-pay Britain's debt for defending them in the French and Indian wars. Other causes of the War of Independence were the Boston Tea Party when huge quantities of tea were overturned into Boston Harbor because of rage towards heavy taxation, and the Boston Massacre where British soldiers fired upon the crowds. These events united the people against the British. The Thirteen Colonies went to war and finally won their independence from Britain. History refers to the period before the British lost her American colonies in the War of Independence as the First Empire. From then onwards the British Empire is referred to as the Second Empire.

Scarcely was the War of Independence over – as if there had not been enough fighting - than the newly formed United States went to war again with England. The US under the presidency of Madison, declared war and immediately attacked the British in Canada for the purpose of gaining more land and also to cut off the British supply lines to the Indian tribes. The major cause of this war was really impressment. The British ships had been attacking US vessels, boarding them and kidnapping as many sailors as they could, forcing them to serve on their vessels as, apparently, they were short of manpower. The Canadian offensive came to naught as the US men were driven back. The British then landed on the Chesapeake Bay, marched on Washington and burnt down the White House. They then advanced on Baltimore. The attack on Fort McHenry was witnessed by Francis Scott Keyes which caused him to write "The Star Spangled Banner", giving us our national anthem.

Now that the American Colonies was a lost cause Britain began to interest herself in India. She started off by developing a few trading stations in the Indian sub-continent. Robert Clive was given the leadership of an expedition to take Calcutta, which he did and fortified it. He made Britain the unrivalled major power in India after driving out the French. In the early 20th century India demanded independence. Realizing that it would not be possible to drive the British out of India. Mahatma Gandhi introduced passive resistance as a means of countering British control in their refusal to grant independence. Gandhi who practiced law in South Africa had introduced passive resistance there in order to fight South African racism. The British slaughtered the Indian resisters at Amritsar in 1919 when there was a disturbance by a crowd of Sikhs and a British general gave orders for his troops to shoot. Three hundred and seventy-nine people were killed. This was after one million Indians had fought on the side of Great Britain in World War I and given the lives of sixty thousand men!

In the course of time Canada, Australia, New Zealand and South Africa received Dominion status within the British Empire. Cecil John Rhodes, the great imperialist who was Prime Minister of the Cape Province in South Africa, dreamt of the entire continent of Africa as a British colony and tried to succeed in developing a Cape-to-Cairo railway line – that is, a connection from the southern tip of Africa to the far distant north of the continent, traveling only on British territory. It almost came true!

After the Treaty of Berlin in 1880 many European countries joined in the Scramble for Africa with the outward pretense of improving the lot of the African, but, in reality, it was for markets, minerals and financial profit. Britain was in the forefront of grabbing territory, with France, Germany and Belgium not too far behind.

There are those who say that the British Empire was a force for improving the lives of their subjects. They brought religion, technology, morality, justice and education to those who had never experienced these advantages of civilization before. These were people who believed in shamanism and ancestral worship. The Age of Enlightenment and the Industrial Revolution had bypassed them. The art of writing and the use of the wheel had been foreign to them. As members of the British Empire many Africans now received education at British schools and newly built universities in their own lands, whereas without the British assistance most of them probably would never have received any education at all. The British introduced government and just laws; they improved the infrastructure, transportation and modernized their societies. They gave them democracy.

Yet there are others who maintain that the British also introduced slavery; they took land away from the natives, they allowed many to die of starvation especially where there was famine, and they killed many of their subjects. What appeared to be altruism on the outside was often discolored by the profit motive. Robert Clive who delivered India to Britain, became a wealthy man in India. Cecil Rhodes, the British imperialist, owned diamond mines in Kimberley, South Africa and founded the De Beers Mining Company; he was one of the richest men in the world. Many others became millionaires as a result of colonialism.

After winning World War II Britain was in financial distress aggravated by the war debt. Winston Churchill was not re-elected and a Labor government came into power. Individual countries of the British Empire were calling for their independence. There was unrest in the Empire. Between the two World Wars, Ireland had fought for its independence and, excluding Northern Ireland, became a free country. After World War II Jomo Kenyatta in Kenya and Kwame Nkruma in Ghana resisted British imperialism and gained freedom for their people. One by one African colonies gained their independence as did India and Pakistan. Mahatma Gandhi's passive resistance movement seemed to have finally worked. East and West Pakistan split off from the rest of India as a homeland for the Muslims of India. Middle Eastern nations, such as Iraq, Syria, Egypt and Trans-Jordan, countries that had been made mandates of Britain or France after World War I now became independent states. One country of the British Empire, the Republic of South Africa, was expelled from the British

Commonwealth because of its policy of apartheid, a policy of treating the Black section of the population unequally, with restrictive laws and social separation while not allowing most of the Black population to rise beyond the poverty level; nor did they have the right to vote. They referred to the system as "equal, but separate" whereas it was really "separate, but unequal".

The British Empire, like all previous Empires of the past, broke up. Britain, who had been victorious in World War II was now having trouble with the peace. Winston Churchill, who had held the fragile Allies together during the Nazi sweep through Europe and the Battle of Britain until the US came into the war, was defeated in the British elections as though he was not appreciated for his heroism in "standing alone", which saved the world by from Nazism. Countries that were members of the British Empire have remained as friends in a loose bond called the British Commonwealth who meet every few years in order to discuss common matters, but it has no connection to the Empire of old. Each country of the old British Empire is totally free, and the British Commonwealth is more like an Alumni or Friendship Club.

Britain, as though lacking friends, joined the European Community in 1973, but has since left it (in 2020) mainly because of immigrants coming from outside, entering Europe and then coming into Britain through porous borders. She also wanted her own privacy and freedom. Britain had always been a proud and independent nation, and Britons had always been nationalistic. Brexit – the name given to Britain's exit from the European Union – will surely weaken the European Union which has tried to put an end to all wars in a continent where war had always been a way of life.

THE FRENCH EMPIRE

There was a French Colonial Empire which started way back in the 16th century under the Bourbon kings. French ships sailed to the Caribbean and India. Motivations for forming an empire were mostly for trade, initially the fur trade, and for spreading Catholicism. By the 17th century it was the second largest empire in the world – only the Spanish Empire was larger. In North America Samuel de Champlain took over Quebec and later in the century Acadia was founded in the surroundings of the St. Lawrence River. The French lost most of their North American colonies to Britain as a result of the Seven Years War starting in 1756. This was a war fought both in Europe and North America. At first France, fighting with North American natives, seemed to be making headway in Canada and the Ohio River Valley, but then the British marched on Quebec and French forts in Ohio. At the Treaty of Paris which ended the war Britain was given Canada, but France made out fairly well in the Caribbean.

Louisiana had a history of being exchanged a few times between France and Spain, finally ending up in French hands, but Napoleon sold it to Jefferson in 1803 when he saw how difficult it would be to maintain a single colony so far away, especially since Haiti had won its independence and Canada had become British a long time ago. There was less reason for France to be colonizing in North America.

Under Napoleon Bonaparte, towards the end of the French Revolution, France became the leading power in Europe. This lasted from 1804 when Napoleon was crowned as Emperor until 1815 when he was defeated at Waterloo by the British under the Duke of Wellington and the Prussians under Marshall Blucher. Most of Europe was under Napoleon's control during that era. Austria, Prussia, Northern Italy and Poland fell to his forces. Spain and Portugal, assisted by Britain, fought a long war against him in the Peninsular War. He poured his troops across the Russian border, where the Russian troops fought a scorched-earth battle against him, leaving very little food and resources to Napoleon's men during a cold and bitter icy winter. Napoleon's troops finally had to withdraw from Russia. This scene was repeated over a hundred years later by the Nazi Wehrmacht in World War II when they invaded Russia and, too, were forced to retreat.

Napoleon was not all bad. He introduced the Code Napoleon to France and the lands that he subjugated. He also brought in to effect trial by jury and legal divorce, abolished the feudal system and freed peasants from serfdom, although the Code gave more power to the man as head of the family. Much of the Napoleonic Code is still practiced in France today.

At last, here was a leader who seemed to be helping the Jews – something that was seldom seen before. Napoleon emancipated the Jews. Jews in France and in Napoleonic Europe were granted equality with all citizens. The ghetto walls came tumbling down. No longer were the Jews prohibited from owning property, restricted from worship or prevented from participating in professions from which they had been barred. Some critics have said that Napoleon did not particularly like Jews. He really wanted them to disappear by assimilation and be like everybody else, and in this manner, they would dissolve as a race, become lost in the crowds around them. He forbade them from practicing usury, so that they would not stand out as being different, and asked them to give themselves French-sounding names or names from the land in which they resided. German Jews thanked him for emancipating them. At the end of the reign of Napoleon the same old discrimination returned to Europe. Napoleon was defeated in 1815, putting an end to his days of glory and France's First Empire.

The French decided to re-build their Empire after 1850, but they diverted their attention to Africa, East Asia and the South Pacific. They spread Catholicism and the French language, and increased their overseas trade. They forced all slaves to be converted to Catholicism. They considered their work to be a civilizing mission, and they brought in equality and justice.

The Second French Empire existed under Napoleon III from 1852 to 1870. He was the nephew of Napoleon Bonaparte, and had been declared President of the French Republic in 1852. Soon after he was elected he dissolved the National Assembly, creating a coup d'etat and making himself emperor.

He set about expanding the French overseas empire. He brought large territories under French control, such as Algeria, Indo-China and South Pacific Islands, including Fiji. He developed a great friendship with the Emir in Algeria and said that Algerians were a part of France. He allowed Algerians who wished to live in France to do so.

While the United States was involved in a Civil War there was trouble across its southern border in Mexico. Mexico had financial problems and was borrowing money from France, Britain and Spain. Juarez, the Mexican leader, could not see how the country's debt could be re-paid so he decided not to re-pay it. Britain, France and Spain sent forces into Mexico either to ensure re-payment or to occupy portions of the country as an exchange. Abraham Lincoln stated that he was very unhappy to see the European nations so close to his borders, especially as there was a dangerous civil war occurring in his country. Spain and Britain decided to return home with their task unaccomplished, but Napoleon III's French troops stayed on, continued the fight and took over the country. In fact, after defeating the Mexicans Napoleon III invited Maximillian III (an Austrian Habsburg) to come and be the Emperor of Mexico, which he did. His rein did not last long as Juarez finally re-took his land and had Maximillian executed.

The end of Napoleon III arrived when he was defeated by the Germans in 1870 at the Franco-Prussian War. Otto Von Bismarck was too smart for him. Alsace and Lorraine were returned to Germany, Napoleon III left France and sought refuge in England where he died three years later.

In 1859 the French started building the Suez Canal under Ferdinand de Lesseps, so that ships going to the Orient could take a short cut instead of having to sail around the southern tip of Africa. This was a great boon for shipping, saving much time and fuel in traveling. For over eighty years the Suez Canal was under the joint ownership of Britain and France until Gamal Abdul Nasser of Egypt occupied it and took over the controls in 1956.

The French Empire extended into World War II. The Nazis invaded France and occupied it in 1940, but allowed the southern area of France, known as Vichy France, to be run by the Petain government. Vichy France also took command of the French navy and her outlying colonies. This allowed Germany more freedom to send its troops to other battle-grounds as required. However, Charles de Gaulle, the leader of the Free French forces, kept whittling away at the Vichy government by taking over many of the French colonies. He intended using them as a spring-board to liberate France from the Germans – but the Allied forces did that for him. However, the French Empire had already started falling during World War II. Japan took over Indo-China, Britain was forced to enter into Syria and Lebanon for strategic reasons while the US invaded Morocco and Algeria. After World War II decolonization continued. Algeria demanded and grabbed independence, as did Madagascar. In French Indo-China (which had been returned to France after the war) Vietnam defeated the French forces at Diem Bien Phu (Japan returned her conquests at the end of World War II). Today France possesses a few overseas islands which have representation in the French Assembly, but there is no longer a French Empire. The history of the French Empire has taken the path of all empires.

There are no large empires any more. One can hardly call the United States an Empire. It is a federation of 50 states with a few outlying possessions. Slavery, colonialism, subjugation of peoples and races are a thing of the past even though there are a few dictators in the world today who glance an inquisitive eye and whet their appetites upon certain weaker nations from time to time. Fortunately, the people of the world are calling for equal rights, freedom and independence amongst all. Organizations, such as Civil Liberties Unions, NAACP, world bodies, such as the United Nations and NATO, will hopefully protect weaker and less armed nations. Perhaps one day we might become more protective and less brutal to each other.

WARS TO END ALL WARS

W HAT WAS THE CAUSE OF World War I? Most history students would say that it was caused by the assassination of Archduke Franz Ferdinand of the Austro-Hungarian Empire. Gavrilo Princip, a Serb, committed the murder of the Archduke and his wife in Sarajevo, Bosnia. That simplified answer might have been the casus belli, the spark that set Europe on fire, but there were many other causes that led up to the war. It is unlikely that one assassination by a possibly deranged person could set off such a conflagration and destroy so many millions of people. The truth is that Europe had been preparing for a war for a number of years before the Archduke's assassination. Europe was heading towards a climax.

By the beginning of the twentieth century the continent of Europe consisted of six Empires, each claiming to be the alpha Empire, and each planning on expansion. There were the German Empire, the Austro-Hungarian Empire, the Ottoman Empire, the Russian Empire, the French and British Empires. Never before had there been so many mighty empires in Europe at the same time. This rivalry was causing increased militarism, nationalism and imperialism among the people on the continent. It was inevitable that with so many Empires something had to give! There would have to be a clash. It was more than a clash – it was a crash!

Each Empire had its own problems, which impinged upon some of the other Empires. The Germans wanted a larger and stronger union; perhaps it was a dream of the days of the Holy Roman Empire. The French wanted revanche (revenge) from Germany for the loss of Alsace and Lorraine in the 1870 war against Prussia. The Russians wanted to unite all Slavs (the Serbs were also Slavs) under her leadership; this bothered the Ottomans and the Austro-Hungarians. The British wanted to rule the high seas unobstructed in order to keep in touch with their overseas possessions, which they hoped would grow further in size. All were jealous of the British and French ownership of distant lands. The Ottomans (sick man of Europe) were having problems with their subjects, far-flung across the globe and demanding independence while their leaders could not control the complaints against them because they were busy fighting amongst themselves. The Balkan states wanted independence from the Ottomans. Both Russia and Austro-Hungary had ideas - different ideas - to wrest the Balkans from the Ottomans. Bismarck said it long ago – the Balkans will be the powder keg that will cause Europe to erupt into a war.

The Entente Cordiale was a treaty between Britain and France whereby each would come to the aid of the other if attacked. Russia joined in the Treaty in 1904, making it into the Triple Entente. Since the time that Russia was defeated by the Japanese in the Russo-Japanese War of 1904 she had been considered a weak and slow-moving giant.

Germany was obviously going to be a major player when the war would finally be fought. General Alfred von Schlieffen was an officer of the German High Command, and he acted as the conductor of the orchestra. He foresaw a problem of fighting a war on two fronts at the same time involving France and Britain in the west and Russia on her eastern border, so he devised a plan that would save the Germans from fighting on both fronts at the same time. Instead of entering France through the well-developed fortifications on the Franco-German border Schliefen's Plan would bypass the French fortifications, and German troops would enter France through Belgium, a neutral country with poor defenses and a limited army. This, he thought, would cause Germany very little trouble. Unfortunately for Schlieffen the Belgians already had an agreement with the British that if attacked Britain would come to their rescue. In six weeks, Schliefen said, France would be defeated, and then the entire German force could concentrate on Russia, the slow ineffective giant.

At the same time Kaiser Wilhelm II had dreams of a large navy, which would greatly enhance Germany's strength. He desired to build a navy as large as his grandmother had under her command. His grandmother was Queen Victoria, the British monarch, who was not only related through marriage of her granddaughters to the German Kaiser, but also to the Czar of Russia. Queen Victoria had nine children and 42 grandchildren. Seven members of her family sat on European thrones – Russia, Germany,

Britain, Greece, Romania, Spain and Norway. It could almost appear that Europe was one happy family! Far from it!

World War I commenced with Austro-Hungary going to war with Serbia. Russia immediately mobilized in order to assist Serbia. France was already mobilized, knowing that she would have to be ready to assist the Russians. Germany told Russia to de-mobilize. She refused, leading Germany to declare war on Russia. Thereupon Hindenburg advanced on Russia, causing France to enter the war.

Following the Schlieffen Plan, Germany attacked Belgium on August 4th, 1914. Matters were not so easy because the Belgians with British help would not let them get through to France. Britain and France joined in the fray at the Battles of the Marne, which was the last river before Paris. It had to be won in order to block the route to Paris. If it had not been won it would have probably meant that the war would soon be won by the Germans.

Schliefen had predicted that the Germans would be in Paris in 45 days, and then most of the troops could be transferred to the Russian front where the Russian troops were considered to be no match for the Germans. He was wrong. The Russians attacked East Prussia while the Germans were held up in Belgium and were unable to be transferred to the Russian front.

Verdun, in 1916, was a problem as the Germans set up a huge onslaught against the French. When Germany attacked at Verdun Britain set up another battle front at the River Somme causing Germany to send many Verdun forces to help out at the Somme, thus relieving the French at Verdun. There were at least one million casualties on both sides as the Allies checked the German advance.

Before the war ended 32 nations had become involved in World War I.

There was no way for the French and British to send supplies to help Russia over land with Germany lying between them. Aid could have been delivered through the Black Sea if it were not controlled by the Ottomans. They used the Black Sea as though it was their own private lake. The Ottomans refused an early demand by the Allies to expel German military and naval missions. Instead, they sank a Russian ship and attacked Russian Black Sea ports causing Russia to declare war on them. Thus, the Ottomans fought on the side of the Central Powers as a continuation of their friendship towards Bismarck and their long-standing history of wars with and animosity towards Russia. They threatened to attack the Suez Canal, which was a lifeline for Britain as it was on her sea route to India.

Keeping the British busy in the Mediterranean region was good news for Germany as she preferred less pressure from them on the Western Front. Winston Churchill sent troops, mostly from Australia and New Zealand, to Gallipoli on the coast of Turkey for the purpose of eliminating Turkey from the war totally and opening up the Dardanelles so the British navy could enter the Black Sea and send supplies to Russia as there was no other easy way to do so. It turned out as having been a big mistake because the Allied forces were soundly defeated by the Turks at Gallipoli and suffered numerous casualties. Churchill received a great deal of blame for the heavy losses in manpower and materiel, and the negative effect upon the morale of the Allies.

The Turks had an ongoing fight with the British in other areas of the Middle East. They lost 800,000 men during the war due to battles, illness, famine and internal massacres. They fought in Palestine, Egypt, Mesopotamia and Persia. Lawrence of Arabia (an Englishman) fought with Arab forces against the Ottomans. This was essentially a war of independence for the Arab states, encouraged by the British, to break away from Ottoman dominance. The Turks could not forget what they called the betrayal by Britain and France through the Sykes-Picot Agreement. While the war was still raging Britain and France prematurely divided up the Ottoman Middle Eastern territory between themselves, as though the war was over and Turkey had already been defeated.

Most of the battles of the war in Europe existed as trench-warfare on the Western Front in France and Belgium. There was not much movement on the Front. Both sides settled in and fought under the protection of the trenches. Wars had changed since the nineteenth century as infantrymen out in the open were now defenseless against the bombardments from massive cannons, "Big Berthas' and a new innovation – planes that were being used to bomb troops and defenses. Horses, too, were extremely vulnerable under these circumstances. Neither side did much in the conquest of territory. It looked like a stalemate.

In 1915 the Lusitania, a British ship, sailing from New York was sunk by a German U-boat off the coast of Ireland. Although it was a passenger vessel with Americans on board it was probably carrying supplies to the

Western Allies, as America had been favoring the Western Allies despite the fact that the US tended to be isolationist. The sinking of the ship was a violation of US maritime rights. However, it was not until the Sussex Pledge was broken subsequently on many occasions that the US entered the war. The Sussex Pledge said that if the U-boats intended to sink a passenger vessel they would have to give the vessel one-half hour notice before doing so in order to save the lives of the passengers. This was one reason that brought the US into the war – the breaking of the Sussex Pledge.

There was another reason for the US going to war against Germany, and that was the Zimmerman Telegram. Zimmerman was a high official in the German High Command. He sent a telegram to Mexico, which was intercepted by the British, stating that if Mexico declared war on the US the Central Powers would see that Mexico would be paid back with the return of Arizona, New Mexico and Texas, which had originally belonged to them. Mexico did not go to war as she did not want to fight the US, but the telegram was enough to upset the U.S.

Woodrow Wilson was thus forced into the war in Europe despite the strong desire in America for isolationism. In the short time that the Americans were involved, having entered the war in the middle of 1917 until Armistice Day in November 1918 they lost 63,000 dead in battle and diseases, including influenza. At the Versailles Peace Conference Woodrow Wilson was suffering from influenza, and was unable to play the part that he intended and that which was expected from him.

However, before World War I was over Woodrow Wilson composed his 14 Point Plan whereby he enumerated what he felt was necessary for a peaceful ending to the conflagration. Perhaps he was more famous for his 14 Point Plan than his input in the Versailles Treaty. He called for democracy among all nations, and diplomacy to prevent wars. He suggested removal of all economic and navigation barriers so nations could trade freely with each other. Belgium, he said, must re-gain its sovereignty, and Alsace-Lorraine must be returned to France. Russia would be welcome to re-join the free nations. The states in the Austro-Hungarian Empire should be free and self-administered while the Balkan nations, too, should be free of Ottoman control. The Ottoman Empire would be disbanded leaving a free Turkey in Anatolia. Poland should become independent. He predicted a democratically run League of Nations. Interestingly enough, the National

Equal Rights League wanted to add a 15th Point "The elimination of civil, political and judicial distinctions based on race or color in all nations". Needless to say, it was not added.

Until the end of World War I a nation called Turkey did not exist. When the war was over the Western Powers proceeded to divide up the Ottoman Empire, leaving behind an abbreviated section of the old Empire, which was basically Anatolia, and that was to be Turkey. Towards the end of the war Greek forces attacked Constantinople, thereby starting the Greco-Turkish war. Lloyd George, Prime Minister of Great Britain, had promised Greece territorial gains at the expense of the failing Ottoman Empire. Anatolia had been a part of ancient Greece and also a part of the Byzantine Empire with Constantinople as its capital. The day after the Armistice in November of 1918 the Allied forces came to the rescue of Greece and occupied Constantinople, sending ships to the Dardanelles and the Bosporus.

Britain had promised the Arabs that they would be granted an independent Arab state if they helped drive out the Ottomans. They fought under Lawrence of Arabia. The British made another promise to the Jews in the Balfour Declaration saying that they would do all in their power to establish a national home for the Jews in Palestine. However, Britain and France had already agreed upon carving up the Arab states amongst themselves, as clearly stated in the Sykes-Picot Agreement, Britain gaining the mandate of Palestine, Trans-Jordan and Iraq while France received Syria and Lebanon as mandates. The Arabs felt cheated as they did not gain their freedom, and the Jews had to wait another thirty years before receiving their own land.

The Western Powers occupied different parts of Anatolia, with Greece and other lands wishing to grab a portion of the new Turkey. However, Mustafa Kemal was able to handle the situation brilliantly and drove off all the grabbing hands. The Treaty of Lausanne of 1923 recognized the Republic of Turkey as the successor to the Ottoman Empire. Mustafa Kemal became the first president of the new Republic of Turkey. He named himself Ataturk. He Westernized an Asian Islamic nation, who were originally Tatars and Turkmen, and made it a secular country, got rid of the fez, chose the Western alphabet for reading and writing in his country, and although he remained a member of the

Islamic Faith he separated government from religion and generally toned down Islamic influences.

From whence came Kemal Ataturk? He was a Young Turk. Who were the Young Turks? It all goes back to the 16th century when in Smyrna (now Izmir), Turkey a Jewish child was born, Shabbatai Zvi. When he grew up he became a rabbi, and soon he claimed to be the Messiah. Unlike some false messiahs before him much that he said was believed by most of the people and ratified by many prominent rabbis. Not only Jews and wise men, but even Muslims and Christians believed that he may be the genuine Messiah; not only in Turkey, but his fame was spreading throughout the known world. He told the Jews from everywhere that he would lead them all back to Jerusalem. This was at a time when the world seemed to need a Messiah, and many leaders of different religions were predicting a possible Messianic arrival. Muslims, too, were expecting the Mahdi. Some Jews removed the roofs or other obstructions from their houses as they wanted to be aware if there should be some sign from the heavens that the Messiah was about to lead them to Jerusalem. The Ottoman government did nothing to hinder Shabbatai Zvi because they were not sure whether he was the true Messiah or not. When Shabbatai told the Jews not to pay their taxes as they would soon be leaving for the Holy Land, the Sultan drew a 'line in the sand'. He would not tolerate Shabbatai's interference in his handling of the Caliphate by withholding taxes from a large portion of the population.

He immediately had Shabbatai taken into custody. Then the Sultan gave him a choice – either convert to Islam or accept death as a punishment for encouraging so many people to defy the law of the land. To the surprise of the entire world Shabbatai chose Islam. Here was a rabbi who chose Islam over and above the God of Israel! He lost most of his followers and became known as the False Messiah, but a hard core of his greatest admirers remained, as his disciples believed that there must be a reason for his actions. He probably wanted to unite Judaism and Islam so that both great religions could live together under the same God, they rationalized. When Shabbatai died those true believers continued to follow him as a sect. They are known as the Donmeh, meaning 'apostates' in Turkey, but with a pejorative twist. Apart from Jews, there were also some followers of Islam who joined the Donmeh. The Donmeh claimed to belong to Islam just as Shabbatai had converted to Islam, but they still secretly prayed to the Jewish God in Hebrew in their homes, while on the outside they resembled other Islamists. Future generations of the Donmeh were looked upon as part of the general Islamic population, but they only married within their own sect and did not wed Jews or Muslims. They existed mostly in Thessaloniki (second largest city in the Ottoman Empire) and Izmir – and there are still a small number who exist in Turkey until this day.

So why am I diverting to this piece of history? Because the Young Turks were derived from the Donmeh and attended Donmeh schools! Kemal Ataturk, too, was a Young Turk and went to a Donmeh school in Thessaloniki. It was the Young Turks who drove out the Caliphate and were probably responsible for the decimation of the Armenian population during the First World War, and it was Kemal Ataturk who became the first leader of the modern Turkish Republic – all from the followers of the False Messiah, a Jew!

In 1923 the Greeks and the Turks, through a suggestion by Ataturk, made an agreement for a population exchange – Greeks in Turkey would be able to return to Greece while Turks in Greece would return to Turkey. This simple population exchange enabled many thousands of Jews to leave Greece and arrive in Turkey, thus saving their lives as fifteen years later Adolph Hitler while inflicting the Final Solution on the Jews, also took the lives of tens of thousands of Greek Jews. Many of the returnees from Greece during the population exchange were Jews and members of the Donmeh from Thessaloniki, who most certainly would have been massacred by the Nazis if not for the Ataturk exchange.

In February 1917 the Communist revolution commenced in Russia. Czar Nicholas II abdicated and Kerensky led the first phase of the Russian Revolution taking over the provisional government while Russia was still at war against Germany and her Allies. German authorities allowed Lenin who was in exile in Switzerland to go back to Russia by train so that he could get Russia out of the war, which would leave the Germans only one Front to battle. The Bolsheviks soon ousted Kerensky, and under Lenin made peace with the Central Powers at the Treaty of Brest-Litovsk in 1918, with Russia ceding territory to Germany, Austro-Hungary and the Ottomans. Poland, the Baltic States, Finland and Georgia became free. The czar and his Romanov family were exiled to Siberia and later killed.

In 1918 the Central Powers collapsed. Bulgaria and the Ottoman Empire dropped out of the war. There was an armistice in November of that year, and Germany claimed that she would not have lost the war if the criminals at home had not pushed the new Weimar Republic into calling for peace. The Kaiser abdicated and went to Holland where he lived until 1941, well into World War II.

At the Treaty of Versailles Italy who had originally joined up with the Central Powers and then left them and joined the Entente Powers because they were not attacked (they had joined the Central Powers on the proviso that they would fight only if they were to be attacked), demanded Trieste and the Dalmatian coast-line. The Prime Minister of Italy, Orlando, walked out of the discussions because the three main powers felt that their demands were excessive. Clemenceau, wanting revenge requested 33 billion dollars from Germany, Alsace and Lorraine and a buffer zone between France and Germany. All his demands were granted. Britain's desire was to enlarge her Empire and wanted her navy to be the greatest so as to connect with the outlying lands of her world-wide Empire. The League of Nations was formed, but Woodrow Wilson, the founder of this body, was unsuccessful in getting his own country to join. Henry Cabot Lodge opposed him, because if Europe became involved in another war, he said, then the US would have to fight all over again. Congress agreed with Lodge, leaving the League of Nations as a body with bark, but only a little bite. Although it had good intentions the League turned out to be largely ineffective. It was obviously weakened by the absence of the US.

Four Empires were destroyed at the Treaty of Versailles. Germany, Turkey, Austro-Hungary and Russia were left without their Empires. The Middle East, following the Sykes-Picot Plan, was divided between the only two remaining Empires, Britain and France. Armenia became a separate state while the Kurds received nothing. German colonies in Africa went to Britain. Yugoslavia became a new country receiving a hodgepodge of Serbian lands combined under one leader. Czechoslovakia also became a new country with a banding together of Czechs, Slovaks and Moravians. The Saar Basin was left to choose its own fate; they chose Germany rather than France. Austria became an entity of its own while losing its Hungarian attachment. Romania received a part of Hungary. Queen Wilhelmina protected Kaiser Wilhelm who was living in the Netherlands and would not extradite him to the Allies for war crimes. Japan who had a treaty with Great Britain since 1902 occupied some Russian islands in the Pacific towards the beginning of the war and assisted with Allied shipping in the Mediterranean during the war. She was granted islands in the Pacific at the Peace Treaty. She also wanted China, but failed to receive such a magnificent gift.

Germany maintained that she did not lose the war; she said that she lost the peace. Actually, she lost the war and the peace. The Treaty of Versailles had all the ingredients necessary to cause another war. Apart from the massive cost of reparations she was to pay to France Germany was also forbidden from building up a new army. Germany was left with little hope, a huge debt, a wrecked economy and severe depression.

There seemed to be no hope for a fallen Germany, struggling to get up from the ground after such a huge knock-out blow until Adolph Hitler arrived, He promised to bring life back into Germany. He was hailed as a hero because of his promise to disobey the Treaty, and was legally elected as Chancellor of Germany in 1932. He replaced the Weimar Republic which ruled after the abdication of Kaiser Wilhelm II. He set about defying the Versailles Treaty and altering the future for Germany. He was the man of the moment. The population flocked to him as though he were the Messiah. He was not German, but Austrian, and only acquired German citizenship prior to becoming Chancellor in the 1930s.

During this period many countries in Europe had been taken over by strong leaders, such as Lenin in Russia, Salazar in Portugal, Franco in Spain and Mussolini in Italy. All were examples for Hitler to try to emulate, but he went further than any of them. Apart from the Treaty of Versailles and the weak state of the League of Nations, what else caused the mighty conflagration which was World War II? The US, Britain and France allowed Hitler to commit all his invasions and atrocities without any objections prior to World War II; this was known as appeasement. At the same time Germany and Japan were building up their armies very rapidly while the Western Powers sat by without applying any counter-measures. They just sat by hoping that with time this, too, would pass.

The first thing Hitler did was to cancel the war debt imposed upon Germany by the Treaty of Versailles. Nobody said a word. Then he started building up the army and navy which had been forbidden by the Treaty, but nobody stopped him. Hitler then marched into the demilitarized Rhineland, and everybody stared and nobody said anything. Alsace and Lorraine had been returned to France by the Treaty, and this remained a pain in the neck to Hitler. However, he promised that he would make sure that they would be returned later. In 1938 the world witnessed the Anschluss which was the bloodless takeover of Austria – again another break in the Versailles Treaty whereby it was stated that Germany was not to invade Austria – but again nobody stopped him. In 1939 Germany invaded the Sudetenland, a portion of the newly formed country of Czechoslovakia, mostly populated by Germans. Thereafter the rest of Czechoslovakia was invaded. All this time the Western powers remained quiet and allowed Germany to acquire these lands without a whimper, possibly because of guilt knowing how cruel and severe the Treaty of Versailles had been upon Germany, but also because they did not want to get involved in another war. The Great War of 1914-1918 had exhausted the nations, and was too expensive in lives and finances. All polls taken at British colleges had one conclusion – the men of military age did not want to go to war. These acts of appeasement continued and nobody tried to stop Hitler.

Neville Chamberlain, prime minister of England returned from Munich after the Sudeten crisis waving a piece of paper in his hand, saying "Peace in our time", and some people unwisely thought that was the end of Germany's demands. Apart from the harshness of the Treaty of Versailles, Germany wanted lebensraum (breathing space) and wanted to dispose of, what she called subhuman beings such as Jews and gypsies, not only in Germany but also in the whole of Europe.

West Prussia had been removed from Germany by the Treaty. It had been given to Poland, while East Prussia remained a part of Germany but was disconnected from it. Germany desired a link with East Prussia.

The Von Ribbentrop-Molotov Pact was a non-aggression pact signed between Germany and Russia in 1939; this surprised everybody. Molotov was not Jewish, but his wife was. Hitler and Communism were arch-enemies, but together they signed the Pact and together they marched into Poland, sharing the spoils. France and Britain had a treaty with Poland to protect her if invaded. Both countries declared war on Germany after the invasion, but nothing was done by the Allies to uphold Polish independence as it was too far, and situated on the other side of Germany.

The Allies, too, were unprepared for war. However, it must be remembered that when the Battle of Britain took place many months later the Free Poles were at hand to help in the defense of Britain.

It was too late to save Poland, but now that Britain and France had entered the war they dare not lose it. Civilization was at the cross-roads. The choice was obvious. Europe, and perhaps the world, would either lose the war and be ruled by a savage dictator or win it and live in peace. World War I was not able to end all wars; perhaps the Western Powers had been given one more chance to do so. The next few months were quiet, except for U-boats in the Atlantic sinking Allied ships with supplies coming in from the US.

After the lull Germany invaded Denmark, Norway, the Netherlands and Belgium, ending up in France. No trench warfare; only what they called blitzkrieg! In a few months Germany had control of most of Europe, including France which was divided into the Northern German- directed area and a Southern portion – Vichy France (not under direct control of Germany). Marshall Petain, an old French war hero from World War I was placed in command of Vichy France by the Germans, but answered to the German High Command. He was allowed to control the French Empire and Navy, making it easier for the Germans who had enough on their hands. At the end of the war Petain was tried as a collaborator by the Allies. His death sentence was commuted by General de Gaulle who considered the patriotic services of Petain in World War I where he came out as a hero.

The British forces could have been annihilated by the German army in France while they were trapped at Dunkirk on their exit from Europe as Germany completed her continental sweep. However, Germany was lenient with the British Expeditionary Force probably because she was hoping to receive British help in the forthcoming attack on Russia, knowing how much the British also detested Communism. Unsuspecting Russia was resting quietly and enjoying the half of Poland which she had recently won. With great fortune the British Expeditionary Force was able to escape intact back to England. Britain now had to survive since most of her Allies were now out of the war. Standing alone England relied on her air force and navy, both of whom performed remarkably well. In order to invade Britain the Germans required control of the English Channel and the skies above Britain. They could not accomplish either. The German Luftwaffe bombed Britain by day and by night, but the British did not surrender. The ceaseless attack from the skies over the steadfast British nation showed the world that they would not give in.

How could an unprepared Britain have survived against the German war machine? The leadership of Winston Churchill, an indomitable spirit of the people, and the RAF were mostly responsible. With the Battle of Britain behind her and Germany losing heart as she saw success slipping away from her, the RAF attacked German cities, like Berlin, Dresden and Hamburg, and destroyed them. The British Navy, of course, policed the waters around Britain and the Mediterranean keeping the free world safe. There was no way that the Germans would be able to invade Britain with a determined RAF and Royal Navy against them.

Italy had an interest in taking over Greece especially since she had already easily conquered Greece's neighbor, Albania, before the war. This would lead her right into the Balkans, so she attacked the Greeks who were very strong in defending their own country. Germany had to come to Italy's rescue before the Greeks would defeat them. At the same time Germany conquered Yugoslavia, giving her control of the Balkans. Tito made a name for himself in the Yugoslav battle, which gave him a boost in becoming the Yugoslav leader at a later date. Britain, who came to help the Greeks, was forced to withdraw her troops to Crete.

Italian forces attacked Egypt from Libya (an Italian colony on Africa's Mediterranean coast), but Hitler again had to help out his Italian allies. He sent Rommel to try and save the Italians from Britain's Montgomery. Rescuing Italy became a familiar story for the Nazis during the war. Here was an ally that had to be propped up!

The Western Powers were saved when America entered the war after the bombing of Pearl Harbor by Japan. America declared war on Japan and the Axis powers. American troops arrived in Britain, and Eisenhower soon entered the North African campaign, but the Axis withdrew from this theater and consolidated their forces in Europe.

Thereupon Germany invaded the Soviet Union along a fifteen hundred-mile Front. Like Napoleon, when he attacked Russia one hundred and thirty years prior to that, Germany was prepared to fight the Russian weather, as well as the Soviet army. Ukraine did not like Stalin because of the imposition of the Five Year Plans which caused them much suffering, so they welcomed the Germans as liberators. The Germans went as far as Leningrad, Moscow and Stalingrad, with millions of men dying on both sides, but this seemed to be as far as they could get. By this time Stalin had re-instated the Soviet generals that he had fired earlier on in his career because he had feared them as possible enemies. The USSR finally got the upper hand, sent the Nazis back in the direction from which they had come and slowly advanced through Russian territory, its satellites and Eastern Europe towards Germany. There was no more retreating and there was no way to stop the Soviets. Then they marched all the way to Berlin.

In the summer of 1941 most of the rest of Europe was under German control. With America now in the war on the side of the Allies Churchill delayed the opening up of the Western Front in Europe in favor of first attacking the soft under-belly of Europe. It was not until September 1943 that the Allies attacked Italy – two years after the German invasion of the USSR. The Allies worked their way up the spine of Italy. In the mean-time Mussolini was toppled by his own people, and thereafter they assassinated him and hung his body on the street for all to see.

June 6th, 1944 or D-Day saw the Allied opening of the Western Front. American, Canadian and British troops invaded Europe. Germany expected an invasion, but was unprepared as to the location of the site of entry. The Western Allies chose the Normandy beaches, and after much fighting they forced their way through France, battling every inch of the way. General de Gaulle led the Allied forces into Paris. Germany made its last heroic stand at the Battle of the Bulge, but the Allies overcame them and marched into Berlin. Eisenhower allowed the USSR to enter first, probably because they had done the most fighting and lost the most personnel. Yes, Germany was defeated. The mighty Empire that Hitler said would last a thousand years reached an abrupt end while still in its infancy. Perhaps one could say that it was stillborn.

At the Potsdam Conference Truman (Roosevelt had already died), Stalin and Churchill decided that the Pacific War must be put to an end rapidly with the defeat of Japan. With the war in Europe over, the Soviets entered Manchuria which was in the hands of the Japanese. It was on the southern border of the Soviet Union, and they conquered it fairly quickly.

Truman was left with a difficult decision – an option of fighting a land war in Japan and losing perhaps hundreds of thousands of men or employing the newly invented Atom Bomb – something he did not wish to use, but it seemed the more favorable of the two choices. An Atom bomb was dropped on Hiroshima and, a few days later, another one was dropped on Nagasaki, killing about 130,000 people altogether. These events resulted in the Japanese calling for peace, thus ending World War II. It cost Japan all its colonies, its leaders were prosecuted for war crimes, while the Emperor was permitted to remain in a ceremonial role. A Diet (legislature) with a bi-cameral parliament was formed, and Japan was not allowed to declare war again. Since then Japan has behaved in an exemplary fashion. Only its relationship with Korea remains rather shaky because of the sex slaves that Japan had created in Korea during their years of occupation. The Koreans cannot forget that dark period.

The Nazi Reich and the Japanese insurgency were Empires of the past. The civilized world had been on the edge of becoming captive to barbarism. There was much joy throughout the world because dictatorship and brutality had been defeated.

JAPAN

Nobody can accuse Japan of ever having participated in the rape of Europe. It had never attacked Europe on its home territory. However, it has fought European Empires in Asia and the Pacific. In World War II Japan attacked and occupied British territories such as Hong Kong, Singapore, Malaya and Burma, as well as French Indo-China. Japan also invaded the islands of the Dutch East Indies (called Indonesia today). They occupied Manchuria, Korea and other areas of China, causing much disruption with heavy losses of property and human life.

One hundred years before the commencement of the Second World War you would probably have been unaware, or only slightly aware of the existence of a land called Japan (Nippon). It was an isolated country at the far eastern side of the globe. Almost no outsiders had ever been there. Japan participated in very little trade outside their own country. Until the 12th century it had been ruled by emperors. Then the shoguns took over; they were military dictators. This was the era of the samurai (military warlords).

In 1854 Commodore Perry of the US Navy entered Tokyo Harbor, firing shells from his gunboat, and he forced upon the Japanese a trade deal with the West. This brought an end to the shogunate and a re-introduction of the power of the emperor. Japan then adopted a Western-style constitution, and from then on became an industrialized nation. She showed a great interest in Western development and proved to be clever at copying what she had learnt. Soon Japan made advances on what she had been taught – a case of where the student out-performed the teacher.

In 1894 Japan went to war with China, and in 1904 she was at war with Russia. She was successful in both wars, gaining land from both countries. She also took control of the Korean Peninsula and Taiwan, unafraid of Chinese resistance which was negligible. By this time it was obvious that Japan was in an expansionist mode. Japan was poor in raw materials and needed to get them for her proposed industrialization. Colonization was one way to get the required raw materials.

Some have blamed Theodore Roosevelt for the aggression of Japan. The Japanese intellect and their ability to copy and learn rapidly caused Roosevelt to believe that Japan would be ideal to act as a powerful leader on the Asian continent, since he was not impressed with Chinese leadership. Apparently, he voiced these opinions to them and sent military experts to train the Japanese army. Japan, too, had little respect for China and could not see them making any progress in building a future for themselves and for Asia.

In 1931 Japan occupied Manchuria. This action was condemned by the League of Nations, and was responsible for Japan's resignation from the League. Japan was becoming a land that was showing industrial growth, competition in the financial world and territorial expansionism.

The bombing of Pearl Harbor in World War II was a continuation of its search for raw materials which was necessary to maintain its expanding economy. One reason for the bombing of Pearl Harbor was that it wanted to prevent the US Navy from interfering in its intended conquest of the Dutch East Indies and Malaya which were rife with raw materials. The harm done to the US Navy by the bombing was considerable. It took the US some time to recover from the blow, but once they were deep in the war the US army and navy gradually persisted in a process of island hopping and pushing the Japanese further and further back. At this stage the war in

Europe was over, and the Allies decided to quickly put an end to the war in Asia with as little loss of life as possible, hence the nuclear bombs dropped on Hiroshima and Nagasaki. Japan called for peace, and General Douglas MacArthur was there to sign the Peace Treaty aboard the USS Missouri.

Strangely, opinions of people and nations have altered. During World War II we looked upon the Japanese as brutal, vicious and uncaring for human life. One need only consider the death marches of Allied troops forced upon them by the Japanese, and many such stories coming out of the war concerning the treatment of war prisoners and occupied peoples. Today we see the Japanese as a kind, gentle, mannerly and peaceful people. Japanese manufactured products were in the past considered to be cheap and inferior as compared to similar articles made elsewhere. However, today Japanese cars, computers, cell phones and cameras have the highest reputation and appear to be as good as the best.

Nevertheless, once again we have witnessed the rise and fall of the Land of the Rising Sun – where the sun seems to have set.

THE COLD WAR

The termination of World War II saw the end of Nazism and, we thought it was the war to end all wars. However, it introduced another problem in Europe. The two major Allies who defeated Germany in World War II found themselves in a war against each other –not a real war, but maybe a virtual war - a war of rivalry, a Cold War. Two different systems, both backed by powerful forces with nuclear capability were facing each other. Communism was now strengthened and the USSR was in an expansionist role. The world had given the Soviets a lot of credit for having defeated the Germans on the Eastern Front and respected them for the huge amount of losses in men, property and materiel that they had undergone. However, the West hated Communism and distrusted the Soviets, knowing that their goal was to spread Communism throughout the world. The Communists equally hated the West and its capitalism. More states were being swallowed up by the Soviet Union. East European countries which were in the Soviet sphere of influence were absorbed into the Soviet Communist Bloc, known as the Warsaw Pact. Germany, the losers of the war, had been occupied and divided into four divisions; one division each to be controlled by USSR, the US, Britain and France. Berlin, the capital, lies in the middle of East Germany which was within Soviet-controlled territory. Berlin, too, was divided into similar divisions. This was the set-up for the Cold War which was responsible for the geo-political tension between the East and the West, and lasted from 1947 until the break-up of the Soviet Union in 1991.

The words, 'Cold War', were taken from the writings of George Orwell, and has since then been the name given to the rivalry between the USSR and the US during the post-World War II period. There was a fear of war breaking out between the allies who had together won the Second World War. It was really a matter of Communism vs. Democracy and Capitalism. It was a fear of mutual destruction, since there had been strides made in the development of nuclear warfare and weapons of mass destruction by both sides. The Allies of World War II were now becoming antagonists, but worse than that – they were nuclear powers. Rivalry occurred in the sphere of propaganda, espionage, even in the arts and science and on the sports fields. Rivalry also existed during small auxiliary conflicts, not involving the major powers, but each major power joined opposite sides in their fight.

The first matter that annoyed the Eastern Bloc was the formation of NATO by the Western Powers as a defense organization against Communism. The Soviets saw NATO as a massive alliance surrounding them and ready to attack. In response they retaliated by forming the Warsaw Pact as a strong counter to the Western Alliance. NATO and the Warsaw Pact faced each other across Germany – or as Winston Churchill referred to it, as the Iron Curtain – the separation between the two ideologies.

In 1948 the Berlin Blockade was started whereby the Soviets would not allow supplies from the West to enter West Berlin, an island within East Germany. The Soviets had demanded reparations from West Germany and that they should remain disarmed, but the Allies wanted Germany to be armed so as to protect Western Europe from Soviet aggression. In fact, West Germany would be the first line of defense and a bulwark against Soviet aggression. In order to overcome the Soviet blockade of West Berlin the US and Britain airlifted essential supplies to West Berlin. This went on for many months until In May of the following year the Soviets shamefacedly ended the blockade. The Soviets had believed that by setting up the blockade the US and Britain might give up the supply line to West Berlin enabling it to enter into the Soviet sphere of influence.

At about this time Mao Tse Tung led his Communist Party in the takeover of China against the forces of Chiang Kai Shek. Naturally the Soviets supported Mao while the Western Powers tried to prop up Chiang. Chiang retreated to Formosa, an island off the eastern coast of China, and today known as Taiwan. The Soviets were pleased to see the expansion of Communism in Asia, since its goal was to spread Communism throughout the world.

In 1950 the Korean War started, and the US went to fight on the side of South Korea against their North Korean Communist brothers who were supported with tanks and other heavy artillery by the Soviet Union and Communist China. The war ended a few years later with North and South Korea remaining as two separate countries, the North supported by the USSR and the South protected by the US. No peace treaty has ever been signed, and the two countries are still officially at war. From time to time there is a flare-up in their relationship and it appears that hostilities could worsen in the future. There is an uneven balance there as North Korea has attained nuclear capability.

The Suez Crisis occurred in 1956 when Gamal Abdul Nasser of Egypt required money to finance the construction of the Aswan Dam. He therefore nationalized the Suez Canal, which was originally built and owned by France and Britain, so that he could collect the tariffs paid by the ships that traversed the canal. This would assist in the financing of the Aswan Dam. The Suez area was immediately invaded by Britain, France and Israel, the latter having had an interest in the area as they had fought a war against the Arab states who attacked them when they declared independence. Israel knew that if Egypt controlled the Suez Canal she would not allow Israeli shipping to pass through. Most of the world oil was shipped through the Suez Canal. Eisenhower had not been forewarned of this invasion. He demanded that all three countries cease the invasion and return home, which they did. A week later Anthony Eden, Britain's Prime Minister, resigned. Nasser was the victor and the hero of Egyptian and Arab nationalism. Israel was prevented from making use of the Suez Canal for her trade and shipping although she was permitted to use the Gulf of

Aqaba, enabling her port of Eilat to be available for international trade. The USSR obviously supported Nasser. At that time the Arab states were pro-Soviet, and they were receiving arms from them. They complained that the US had been assisting Israel against them.

The Cuban Missile Crisis almost brought the Cold War powers close to a real war. After Fidel Castro assumed control of Cuba he aligned himself with the Soviet leaders who assisted him in every way that they could. In 1962 a US spy plane viewed Soviet missiles being set up in Cuba, 92 miles from Florida. These were nuclear-armed missiles. President Kennedy warned the Soviets to remove those missiles or else there would be a total blockade of Cuba. After thirteen days of fear of a nuclear war Khrushchev said that he would remove the missiles if the US did not attack Cuba and if the missiles in Turkey (a NATO ally) aimed at the Soviet Union would also be dismantled. Kennedy agreed, and war was averted.

In 1968 Czechoslovakia was given a new leader, Alexander Dubcek; he was a Slovak, and he planned on lessening the severity of the suffering that the people had endured during the time of the past autocratic government, and he also introduced free speech. The Czechs were celebrating the new freedoms, referred to as the Prague Spring. The Soviets were very unhappy about Dubcek and his plans. They sent in 600,000 troops and made sure that the old system remained intact, bringing the people back to where they had been before the Prague Spring.

The US was having a problem of its own in the 60s. They were supporting the South Vietnamese in a war against the Communists of North Vietnam. The Soviets, of course, were supporting the North Vietnamese. This was a prolonged war where three million people were killed, including 58,000 Americans. The war was very unpopular within the United States where a majority of American citizens were against fighting to solve the internal problems facing an Asian nation. Numerous protests, sit-ins and anti-war demonstrations took place in the US, demanding withdrawal from Vietnam. Many young men refused to go when called up for the army and many left the country. At the same time the US was also having a problem with demands for an increase in civil rights. There were demonstrations, marches and sit-ins. At least three US presidents were involved in the Vietnam War, one of whom (Lyndon Johnson) did not seek re-election because of turmoil in the US and problems emanating from the Vietnam War. The North Vietnamese finally entered the capital, Saigon, and united the country while the US withdrew its forces from South Vietnam.

In 1979 the Soviets invaded Afghanistan in order to prop up the pro-Soviet government that was failing. However, they stayed there many years but could not tame the mujahideen (Afghan fighters) who were fighting them in spurts, stealing their equipment and running back into the mountains where they could not be found. The US was assisting the anti-Soviet Afghan fighters, including the Taliban. Imagine that! – The US supporting the Taliban! Finally, when Gorbachev became the Soviet leader he withdrew his troops as the Soviets had incurred immense losses in men and materiel.

When Mikhael Gorbachev took over the reins of the Soviet Union he introduced glasnost (openness) and perestroika (restructuring). It sounds very liberal and democratic, which it was. Understandably, it helped to bring down the Soviet Union. He wanted to loosen the autocratic form of government and introduce some form of democracy, but the taste of a little freedom was enough to set the revolutionary feeling aflame within the Soviet Republics. Gorbachev said that the old system collapsed before the new one was able to start. He wanted better relations with the outside world. Reagan had spoken of the USSR as the evil empire. Gorbachev took his forces out of Afghanistan, out of the arms race, reduced the militarization and spoke in a tone foreign to that of his predecessors. Poland was the first, through Solidarity, to demand freedom. Then came the fall of the Berlin Wall and the pouring out of East Germans into West Germany! The Velvet Revolution saw a free Czechoslovakia, and this was followed by the separation from the USSR of Latvia, Estonia and Lithuania. The breakaway of the tiles from the Soviet edifice appeared to be endless.

In August 1991 Gorbachev while on vacation in the south of Russia was placed under house arrest. The military and members of the solid Communist base marched on Moscow, but a human chain held them back while Boris Yeltsin, a rising figure in the Communist Party, stood on a tank defying them. The military coup failed. Gorbachev was released from his confinement while more member states broke away from the Soviet Union. Gorbachev resigned and Yeltsin became the new leader of Russia.

Gorbachev announced that this was the end of an era - the Cold War, the arms race, mad militarization, a crippled economy and a time when there was an absence of morality in the land.

Since the end of the Cold War, relationships between the US and the Russian Federation (a few of the old Soviet Socialist Republics stayed with Russia as the Russian Federation) have been cool. The Russian leadership seems to be moving in the direction of the Cold War days even though it is far less intense. The Marxist-Leninist philosophy is, presumably, no longer present as Russia does not have a Communist government or economy. The Cold War brought out the fact that the world has two super-powers, Russia and the USA, even though Russia, today, has only half of the US population since the dissolution of the Soviets. The rivalry continues but the arms build-up, including the nuclear proliferation on both sides has made an all-out war appear less probable as nations might be afraid to start a war that could possibly put an end to our entire civilization.

Just as the Cold War replaced military encounters we might, in the future, be seeing the Cold War being replaced by Ideological warfare. Cyberwarfare may become more prominent among these two giants. We have already seen cyber-attacks at play in the 2016 US elections when the Russians preferred to have Donald Trump as President of the US rather than Hillary Clinton; and we have seen cyber-attacks recently on a number of large US companies stemming from the Russians. We also saw cyberwarfare used when Israel interfered in the Iranian attempt at building a nuclear weapon. This may become a way of fighting a war in the future – more damage done but less in the way of loss of life. This could be accomplished by infecting a computer with malware or hacking. Cyber-attacks can be launched from anywhere in the world. One does not need proximity to the enemy, nor does one need to be a powerful nation to cause damage. Terrorists or a single individual could attack the most powerful nation. A country need not suffer the expense of training, transporting or feeding an army or supply artillery, planes or ships to fight an enemy. All one needs is a computer and its master.

In 2014 President Putin annexed the Crimea which had been a part of the Ukraine, and since then there have been Russian forays and fighting for some other areas in the Eastern Ukraine. Russia has fewer friends in Eastern Europe at present as compared to the post-World War II days when the entire Eastern Europe was under her leadership. Many of Russia's friends of the past have joined NATO and the European Union. They have joined the enemy. The US, too, seems to have fewer friends since the Cold War days probably because the European Union has taken over as the protective shield. Let us say that the motherly arms of the European Union are big enough to care for many lands, which is making reliance on the US less imperative.

After living in the face of wars, invasions, epidemics, destruction and revolutions Europe has finally attempted to solve her problems peacefully. The European Union started in 1951 as the European Coal and Steel Community. It was developed to serve France and Germany for the purpose of making the two countries dependent upon each other so that they would never again be able to go to war against each other. They had been killing each other too often in the past. Out of this wedlock was born the European Union for the purpose of promoting peace. One by one European lands joined this group – even some countries which had previously belonged to the Warsaw Pact - so that today there are 27 members of the European Union, 19 of which employ the euro as a monetary exchange medium. There is a goal to have a unified economic and monetary system with a breakdown of trade barriers. Scientific development is encouraged and there will be environmental protections. They aim to combat discrimination and they wish to put an end to war. There is free movement of people, goods, services and money across all European borders, and passports have been abolished for travel within the lands of the European Union.

Great Britain has been a member of the European Union for decades, but of late has voted in favor of leaving the Union because they wanted better control of immigration and the borders. Britain has always shown a sense of independence. Perhaps being an island has made her isolated and independent. Time will tell whether Brexit (British exit) was a good move for the British people. Time will also tell whether the formation of the European Union has been a positive force for putting an end to the atrocities, hatred, wars and revolutions that have ravaged Europe almost forever. There has never been a time in history when Europeans could have looked forward to a more peaceful future. Carpe diem!

ANOTHER EMPIRE BITES THE DUST

❖

RUSSIA IS THE LARGEST COUNTRY in Eurasia. It covers two continents and six time zones. Throughout many centuries it has been ruled by a czar. Towards the end of the 19th century the ideas of Karl Marx, a German, spread throughout Europe. Marx believed that social classes were the result of a struggle between the capitalists who owned the bulk of the money and most of the assets, and the lower classes who owned next to nothing. The lower classes were oppressed by the capitalists. Capitalists owned the industries but the profits were produced by the poor and hungry workers. Therefore, there should be co-operative ownership by all. Socialism and communism were discussed in intellectual circles, but when talk of it came to Russia the czar refused to share power with anyone. He believed that his sovereignty was given to him by God.

In 1898 the Russian Socialist and Democratic Party decided to go along with Marxism, which was the beginning of Russian, and later, Soviet Communism. However, about five years later there was a split in the Party into Mensheviks and Bolsheviks, the latter being more extreme and not wishing to wait before making changes; they were for world revolution, sooner rather than later. The Mensheviks were more easy-going and they believed that time would bring change.

The Russian Revolution of 1905 was spurred by the Russian defeat in the Russo-Japanese War. There were worker strikes all over the country while poverty was rife. There was a feeling amongst the people that something was radically wrong. The workers minds were full of the new Marxist socialism while they were living under an autocratic regime with no glimmer of hope for the future. The Czar held on to his position after the revolution died down, but he accepted the establishment of a Duma, which was the beginning of a multi-party system. The autocracy of Czar

Nicholas II became a constitutional monarchy. Alexander Kerensky, a socialist, became a member of the Duma.

In February 1917 riots broke out in the streets of St. Petersburg because of the scarcity of food. Russia was in the midst of World War I. The people were suffering at home while their army was losing on the war front. At the same time there was social unrest within the country. Matters worsened and there was further rioting until the czar was forced to abdicate. A Provisional government was formed under Kerensky. Vladimir Lenin had been in exile in Switzerland, but the Germans arranged for him to return to Russia by train for the purpose of him taking over the reins of government and getting Russia out of the war against Germany so that Germany would not have to fight the Allies on two fronts.

This is exactly what happened. After his arrival Lenin staged a coup upon the Provisional government, thus ousting Kerensky and taking over the reins of government himself. He made peace with Germany. Lenin was a Bolshevik who wanted revolution now; there was no time to waste. Communism would have to be instituted immediately and this would have to spread internationally.

A war between Communist Russia and the White Russians followed, lasting from the end of 1917 to 1922. The White Russians consisted of dissidents, czarists, anti-Communists and troops sent in by the US and her Allies who were afraid of the spread of Communism throughout Europe and beyond.

Lenin set out to abolish all symbols and titles of czarism, put an end to ownership of land and estates. He said he was going to introduce civil rights and equality of citizenship to all, male and female genders would be equal, women would get equal pay and be allowed to vote. He formed the Red Army and a Secret Service. Intermingled with the Civil War a reign of terror took place. There was a severe drought and famine in the land. Civil War, drought and famine, it is said, was responsible for 5 to 10 million deaths. Then he set about re-building and recovering the nation.

In 1924 Lenin died. He was supposed to have been followed by Leon Trotsky, his own choice. Instead, Joseph Stalin (who was not born in Russia, but Georgia), with much maneuvering, grabbed the leadership role. Stalin had held a desk position in the Communist Party. He met all the important people and knew everyone. He was able, by cunning and trickery, to get the right people to vote for him. Ruthless cunning guided Stalin's life. Russia was not the paradise that the workers and peasants had been promised. There was collectivization of the workers, work was severe and there was very little gain in working for the State. The Secret Police were not far away, and very active and cruel in handling dissenters. The kulaks were wealthy farmers who had owned and had profited from their land before the Revolution. They opposed Stalin's collectivization, but were soon herded in and sent to Siberia. Many other victims and so-called enemies of the State were sent to Siberia, some of whom were never seen again. Yet the State was depicted to the masses as a new Paradise with a great future ahead. Communism created far more suffering amongst the people than what had existed under the czar.

The USSR was formed in 1922 and consisted of fifteen Soviet Socialist Republics, some from Central Asia (Kazakhstan, Kyrgyzstan, Uzbekistan, Azerbaijan, Tajikistan, Turkmenistan and Armenia), the three Baltic States (Estonia, Latvia and Lithuania), and Russia, Georgia, Ukraine, Belorussia and Moldovia. The country was ruled by a federal government, but Stalin, as the leader of the Communist Party, had total power. He ruled as a dictator despite the existence of a Congress which was powerless. Stalin instituted a number of Five Year Plans which was meant to improve the agricultural production of the country under a system of collective farming. Under Stalin, and especially between 1936 and 1938, there were numerous purges, repressions and tight police surveillance. Suspicion was rife, and nobody knew who was watching their movements, and who was friend or foe. It was often a family member, who should not have been trusted. Prisons were usually fully occupied, and the gulags stretched like an archipelago (apologies to Solzhenitsyn) across Siberia. Many never returned from Siberia as executions were commonplace. It is said that Stalin was probably responsible for more loss of life than even Adolph Hitler. Stalin's paranoia caused him to eliminate his political opponents, doctors, and even generals. As a matter of fact, when Germany invaded the Soviet Union they were able to advance swiftly because Stalin had already eliminated his best generals for fear of any rivalry and opposition from them.

Hitler despised Communism. He accused the Jews for having tried to introduce it into Germany at the end of World War I. He classed them as communists, apart from everything else that he accused them of being. Imagine the consternation of the world when Germany and the Soviet Union signed a Non-Aggression Pact in August 1939 just prior to World War II! This Pact was to last for ten years, and was signed by Molotov, the Soviet Foreign Minister (whose wife was Jewish) and von Ribbentrop, Germany's counterpart. One month later both Germany and the Soviet Union invaded Poland, dividing the territory and the spoils between them. This way Hitler thought that he could attack France and Britain without having to worry about a Second Front from Russia. In less than two years this Non-Aggression Pact was broken when Hitler's armies invaded his Non-Aggression Pact partner, the Soviet Union.

Operation Barbarossa was the code name of the German invasion of the Soviet Union. Britain had survived the Battle of Britain after the fall of France, and showed no signs of surrendering. Hitler would have liked to have defeated the British and then used them to assist him in an invasion of Russia, or at least to stay out of the war knowing that the British were not enamored with communism either. However, this was not to be. After the Battle of Britain Hitler could not foresee a sea-borne invasion of the British Isles, especially as everybody knew that Britannia ruled the waves. He therefore went along on his own. The Nazis moved in on a fifteen hundred mile front from the north of Russia to the Crimean Peninsula. The Germans, invading through Ukraine, were welcomed as saviors, such was their hatred for Stalin and his Five Year Plans, even though Ukraine was a member of the USSR. The Nazis progressed swiftly at first, laying waste to the land and destroying everything before them. They captured five million Red Army men, many of whom were never seen again. Before much time had elapsed, there were 150,000 dead Soviet soldiers. One million Red Army men died in Stalingrad over a period of a few months. It was said that a Russian soldier's life expectancy at the Front was 24 hours. The Soviets lacked good generals because Stalin had ousted them for fear of opposition from them. Stalin was about to abandon Moscow and flee towards the east where a new capital was being set up at Kuibyshev. He was encouraged by his cronies to keep up the fight. The Germans were held up at Stalingrad, Moscow and Leningrad. And then the tide turned. The Soviets did not give up those three cities. Stalin re-appointed the ousted generals in order to strengthen his forces. The Red Army, like a giant, woke up, turned around and began to advance. They pierced the Nazi Front in many areas and did not stop marching until they were in Berlin wielding the Soviet flag at the front of the Reichstag while the Allied forces were still advancing through France. In time they, too, arrived in Berlin.

After World War II the Soviet Union developed the atom bomb, and became one of the two world super-powers, the other one, of course, being the United States. They had feared that they would be left behind in the nuclear arms race, but fortune was on their side.

NATO (or the North Atlantic Treaty Organization) had been formed soon after the war by the United States and the Western European powers in order to prevent Communism from spreading into Western Europe and even beyond that. Greece and Turkey had been aided by NATO when it appeared that Communism was attempting to envelop them. Then the Soviet Union formed the Warsaw Pact (in 1956) whereby she consolidated her position and made sure that Eastern Europe would be a powerful Communist conclave. The Warsaw Pact would counter the power of NATO. Both the Warsaw Pact and NATO perceived each other as enemies even though their countries had been allies during the war.

Yugoslavia was a Communist country allied to the Soviet Union, but Tito was able to keep his country outside the Warsaw Pact, giving him some degree of independence. The inhabitants of the Soviet Union and the members of the Warsaw Pact were pressured into the hatred of Capitalism while anything smelling of Westernization was frowned upon, and religion, too, was taboo. The arts and literature were encouraged to be produced in a Russian nationalistic and patriotic form, and there should be no decadent Western influence.

What happened to the relationship of the Allies – the Soviet Union and the USA - of World War II that defeated Hitler? There were tensions between them, they distrusted each other, and they competed against each other. The long-standing hatred between Communism and Capitalism worsened. There was no physical war between the Soviet Union and the Western Powers, but when a smaller war among other nations developed the Warsaw Pact supported the communists and NATO supported the non-communist side amongst the belligerents. The new relationship was the Cold War, which lasted from 1945 until the break-up of the Soviet Union in 1992.

The Communists were a large bloc. Immediately after the Second World War ended the Soviet Union had occupied Poland, Romania, Czechoslovakia, Hungary, Bulgaria and East Germany. Other Soviet satellites included Albania, Estonia, Lithuania and Latvia. There was also Outer Mongolia that became a Communist state, and in 1948 China became Communist.

At both Yalta and Potsdam Stalin had demanded a free hand in Eastern Europe, and in return promised to have free elections in all the satellite states. Free elections never occurred, and all his satellite countries were ruled by Communist governments with iron hands. It has been much debated whether the Allies should have allowed Stalin such liberties. The whole of Eastern Europe had now fallen to Communism. When Hungary in 1956 and Czechoslovakia in 1963 showed signs of independence, and there was lightening of the Communist cloud over them the Soviets marched in and brought matters back to the way in which they had been. As Winston Churchill stated, there was an Iron Curtain separating the Communist bloc from the rest of Europe.

The Marshall Plan was instituted in order to provide funds for re-building the Europe that was destroyed during the war and to insure Western European democracy against Communism. Actually, NATO had even offered financial aid to the Soviets, but it was rejected.

The Soviets said they needed a buffer zone to protect them against a possible repeat attack from Germany in the future. They said that they wanted to prevent West German Fascists from getting into East Germany, but they really wanted to prevent fleeing communists from East Germany and other satellites from entering West Berlin, so they built the Berlin Wall. Khrushchev said that West Berlin was like a bone in the throat of the Soviets. The West Germans called the Berlin Wall the 'wall of shame'.

Following World War II the Soviets lacked money, machinery and food, despite the fact that the Red Army was the most powerful army in the world. The USSR had suffered more casualties and more property damage than any other country in World War II. How did they handle their impoverishment and their famine, their failing economy and their battered lives? They stripped East Germany of their machinery and grabbed hold of their engineers. They took whatever they could get from their satellite states and started to re-construct the damage wrought by a cruel war rather than receive any aid from the American Marshall Plan. People had been living in bombed-out buildings and holes in the landscape. They had been dying of starvation while others were executed in the purges which Stalin resorted to at the slightest pretext. This applied to those who behaved suspiciously, those who might be dangerous in the future and those artists and writers who pursued their work in a Western-oriented style, as well as people who did not worship Communism and the Motherland.

Then came the Cold War, a war in which no bullets were fired at each other, but nevertheless, lasted forty-five years. Britain and America worried about Soviet dominance in Eastern Europe. Would this be permanent and would it spread throughout Europe and perhaps to other parts of the world, as was the Bolshevik philosophy? The Soviets were afraid of Democracy and Capitalism in the West and jealous of their scientific advances. At the beginning they had feared that America possessed the atom bomb, and she did not share her secrets with her ally, the Soviet Union. Later when the Soviets developed nuclear capability they were willing to confront the West with more confidence. Yet there was a fear by both sides of a global nuclear disaster. The two philosophies seemed to be coming from two different worlds.

I have discussed the Cold War in the chapter titled "Wars to End War", so I will not repeat myself by dealing with the different incidents occurring throughout the Cold War. However, there was extreme rivalry between these two giants with the US supporting its former enemy, Germany, against its former Ally, the Soviets. Strange how things change!

The US and the Soviets did not fight each other, but each took sides – opposite sides – in the conflicts. Even on the sports field they took sides, supporting the team that followed their particular ideologies. If one of them was involved in a conflict the other would back and assist the other side without entering into the fray.

The Truman Doctrine of 1947 was accepted by the Soviets as a declaration of the Cold War. It was expressed by Truman when it appeared as though Greece and Turkey were being threatened by Communism, and it was a call to assist them in order to counter the threat. It warned the Soviets that all attempts at spreading Communism would be opposed by the West. The formation of NATO in 1949, too, was regarded by the Soviets as a threat to them and a solid defense line to control them.

Therefore, they countered with the Warsaw Pact of 1955, which included all the Soviet bloc countries surrounding them, as a buffer against NATO.

The Soviets, forever intending to spread Communism throughout the world – their Marxist mission – were searching for countries where they could introduce their philosophy. They searched the Latin American landscape in South America, the Middle East, Asia and Africa, where colonialism was losing ground and becoming a thing of the past. They had some minimal success. They were delighted when Mao tse Tung took over China, bringing Communism to about a billion people and driving Chiang Kai Shek into the island of Formosa (now Taiwan). The Soviets were China's greatest friend. They sent engineers to China to assist in setting up industry and major factories, including aircraft construction plants. However, by the early 'sixties there was a Sino-Soviet split. The split involved a difference in interpretation and a doctrinal divergence by the followers of Marx. Mao felt that the Soviets were practicing socio-imperialism rather than pure Communism. Khrushchev encouraged the Uyghurs (Chinese Buddhists) to rebel against Mao. The two major Communist countries turned away from each other. In fact, Mao made overtures to Nixon which culminated in a visit to China by Nixon - and a beginning of a new Sino-American relationship.

The end of the Cold War came with the unexpected disintegration of the Soviet Union. Gorbachev became the new Soviet leader in 1985. He wanted to improve the economy which had been failing. One big problem in the Soviets was alcoholism, so he added taxes to alcoholic beverages. With the decreased drinking that followed and concomitant decrease in alcohol taxes which ensued there was less money coming into government funds, and therefore no assistance to the economy. The arms race also placed a burden on the economy so Gorbachev was forced to enter into treaties with the US in order to slow down the race of nuclear and other weaponry. The Afghan War, where the Soviets sent in troops to prop up a failing Communist government, was another drain on the financial state of the Soviets, so he decided to remove his troops from Afghanistan.

Gorbachev introduced glasnost, which is open discussion, and perestroika, meaning re-structuring – a giant step forward for a land where foreign news broadcasts had not even been permitted. This was rather risky in a nation where one was afraid to open one's mouth in case anybody might report you if you said the wrong thing. He wanted to introduce some elements of democracy and loosen some of the constraints of autocracy. A taste of democracy was enough to set up a revolutionary feeling with some of the Soviet Republics.

Boris Yeltsin and Gorbachev started off as friends and worked together, but that relationship soon grew sour. Yeltsin said that glasnost and perestroika were too moderate and he called for a multi-party system and democracy. He became a rebel and anti-establishment, and for the next four years there was a Yeltsin-Gorbachev struggle which played a large part in the dissolution of the Soviet Union. Gorbachev was beginning to lose control of the Soviet people. There was internal unrest and murmurings of independence coming from the Asian Republics where there was also rioting. The Baltic Republics, led by Estonia, were all calling for independence. In Armenia, which had been the most accepting of all the Asian Republics, there were territorial demands from Azerbaijan for Nagorno-Karabakh where many Armenians had been residing. By 1990 six Republics were lost to the Soviet Union – Estonia, Latvia, Lithuania, Moldova, Armenia and Georgia. Reagan had called the Soviet Union the Evil Empire, while Gorbachev tried to undo that impression and improve the opinions of the Soviets in other countries.

Amid the falling apart of the Soviet Union there were problems in East Germany. More East Germans had been escaping into West Berlin and West Germany despite the concrete walls holding them apart. Erich Honecker, the East German leader, resigned. The East German authorities met and discussed the problem of the large number of people escaping from their territories. The man who passed the message on to the broadcasting stations was not at the meeting, but had been given an incomplete report. He told the media that at the meeting it was decided that anybody who wished to visit West Germany may do so. Huge crowds crossed into West German territory. The Berlin Wall fell while the Soviet Union was teetering. In the next few months the Wall was demolished and the road to German re-unification was paved.

To add to the problems Yeltsin resigned from the Communist Party. No important figure had ever before resigned from the Communist Party. In June 1991 Yeltsin, running as an Independent, was elected as President.

Of course, Gorbachev was still General Secretary of the Communist Party, which was a higher position than President of the Soviet Union. All this time the radical reformists were calling for a market economy.

While Gorbachev was on vacation in the Crimea in August 1991 he was apprehended and placed under house arrest. At the same time there was a coup in Moscow where diehard Communists tried to take over the government, being certain that the public would join them, but it was not so. Yeltsin climbed on to a tank and rallied the people against the coup. They tried to arrest Yeltsin, but the people protected him. Needless to say, the coup turned out to be a failure. Gorbachev was released, and both he and Yeltsin continued with their jobs.

However, between August and December 1991, a total of ten republics became independent. In September the Baltic States that were already independent, joined the United Nations. They later joined NATO and the European Union. They joined the enemy! Could you imagine such a change-over! Russia, Belorus and Ukraine formed a loose union, called the CIS – Confederation of Independent States. On Christmas Day, Gorbachev resigned, declaring that his office was extinct, while ceding power to Yeltsin. Gorbachev said "The old system collapsed before the new one had time to start working". The Soviet flag was replaced by the old Russian flag. At this time the Cold War, too, officially came to an end.

Gorbachev's decision to allow free elections was probably one of the main causes of the fall of the Soviet Union. This democratic process was too much for a Communist controlled nation to tolerate. Yeltsin transformed the Communist economy to a Capitalist market economy. The oligarchs entered into the picture and took over financial control to the detriment of the major portion of the population. At that stage there was a Depression over the entire country, worse than the Depression that hit Europe and the USA in the late nineteen-twenties and -thirties.

In 1993 Yeltsin was almost overthrown when he dissolved the Supreme Soviet, but the military saved him from that fate. A year later he invaded Chechnya which had caused much upheaval in Russia for the preceding few years. Chechnya was a part of Russia, and their people had created a number of riots both in Chechnya and other areas of the Soviet Union. Yeltsin's troops brought peace and quiet to the territory in exchange for increased autonomy for the Chechnyans.

Yeltsin displayed little interest in co-operating with the Supreme Soviet, nor they for him. Each introduced laws without discussion with the other. He overcame assassination and impeachment attempts until in 1999 when he resigned. Alcoholism and heart disease finally put an end to his life in 2007. He was very erratic in many of his actions which were not always successful, but he was the one who finally ended the Communist era of the Soviet Union. Nobody else had been able to do so. He said "Communism is a world of fantasy". He introduced civil rights into Russia and was the first anti-Communist leader of the Soviet Union.

Yeltsin recommended Vladimir Putin as his successor. Putin had been an important officer of the KGB. Since his arrival as Russia's leader there has been a diminution of democracy which Yeltsin had introduced. Jailing of political opponents is not uncommon in the Russia of today. There have been tortures and assassinations, as well as poisonings of his enemies. He has introduced legislation against the gay and bi-sexual community in Russia. Accusations have been made that Putin has interfered in the US elections and is still interfering in the manner of cyber-warfare. He did not like the direction that Gorbachev was leading the Soviet Union. He has since stated that the collapse of the Soviet Union has been the greatest geo-political catastrophe of the 20th century.

Within the last few years he has intervened in the politics of Ukraine. He has taken over the Crimean Peninsula and invaded the Eastern Ukraine. He has responded to Assad of Syria by sending troops to Syria and actually improving Assad's position in the on-going civil war by bombing his enemies and strengthening his defenses. Before Putin's troops came to Syria Assad was actually losing the civil war.

It appears as though Putin is trying to re-establish the power of the old Soviet Union. He says that he is not trying to copy US or British democracy, but that he is doing it in the Russian way, which appears to outsiders as a dictatorial way. He seems to be involved with the oligarchs, and it is noted that he is a very rich man. He has enacted laws that would allow him to remain as leader of Russia for many years to come. A fair number of people have been arrested or disappeared or been poisoned by neurotoxic agents, such as the leader of the opposition Party, Navalny, whose life was recently saved in a hospital in Germany. He appears to get rid of his enemies in much the same way as Joseph Stalin did, although perhaps not in such large numbers. The Soviet dictatorship and its Empire are history, but we can see that there are some resemblances to the past still in evidence in present day Russia.

COMING TO AMERICA

MOST HISTORY BOOKS SAY THAT Christopher Columbus discovered America in 1492, even though he was never on the mainland. He actually discovered the West Indies, groups of islands close to Central America. Amerigo Vespucci, a Florentine by birth, sailed on a number of voyages for Spain and later for Portugal between 1497 and 1504, and he is given the honor of having discovered America. On his third voyage he reached the mainland of South America in Rio de Janeiro, and later went south to the Rio de la Plata. He realized that he was not in Asia but in a New World, later named after him, America. Other books will tell you that Leif Erikson, son of Erik the Red, landed on Newfoundland in the year of 1,000, almost five hundred years before Columbus and Vespucci. You might even have read that the Chinese who were great sailors landed on the American continent about seventy years before Vespucci. You might not have read that approximately twelve thousand years ago the American continent was occupied by tribes from Asia crossing over the Bering Straits. They are really the people who discovered America.

When Christopher Columbus arrived in the West Indies on the Caribbean islands there were about 145 million Native Americans living on the American mainland, but by the 18th century, after the invasion of the White people, 90% of them had been exterminated, either having been slaughtered by the newcomers or by having contracted the diseases that these White people brought with them, diseases such as chicken pox, small pox and measles. The natives had no herd immunity to these new maladies since those infections had never occurred amongst them.

Where did the Native Americans originate? The vast majority came from Eurasia. About twelve thousand years ago they crossed the Bering Straits, a channel between Siberia and Alaska, which was probably an over-land crossing during the Ice Age, known as Beringia. Once on the American continent they could go south, east and west with no one to stop them. All they needed was time, and in time they covered the entire North American continent, entered South America and went all the way down as far as Tierra del Fuego at the southern tip of the New World. When Columbus arrived in the West Indies he met the American native there. He referred to them as Indians because he thought that he had reached India. After all, he had been sailing to find a sea route to India.

A small number of Native Americans living in the Amazon region of Brazil have a mysterious link in their DNA connecting them to the Australian aborigines and Papuans. There is no clear-cut answer to this connection unless these Australasians somehow got mixed in with the Siberian emigration parties going over the Bering Straits. We do know, however, that the Polynesians were great boat people, and that they sailed all the way to Easter Island, Hawaii and other Pacific Islands close to the South American continent, so they could possibly have arrived in South America as well; but the Polynesians are different from Australian aborigines who were not known for their sea-faring abilities. This problem, at the moment, appears to be insoluble. The Egyptians, too, were fine seamen and participated in some migrations. We see that the pyramids of Central America have an architectural resemblance to the Egyptian pyramids. The Mayan pyramids tend to be smaller and tend to be surrounded by steps. There may possibly have been other entries to the American continent apart from the Bering Straits. It is hard to believe that there was only one gateway into this huge continent spanning two hemispheres. Living in America was for these Native Americans like living on a different planet. There was no communication with the Old World. They were isolated from the rest of the world. They were unaware of the wars of Europe, the founding of the three major religions, the creations and spread of the vast Empires of Europe and Asia, the cultural advances and the scientific and medical innovations throughout the centuries. Yet in their own way they made inroads into their development as a people until the White Man arrived. The White Man came in the form of Pilgrims, Puritans, Spaniards and Portuguese, followed by more British, French and everyone else who was looking for a new life. Once the White Man arrived life would never be the same again for the Native American.

He was abused and hunted, and he was massacred. He was driven away from his home and his land where he had always felt free, and he was forced to try to start a new life elsewhere. No sooner that he was rejected and ejected he was attacked again, and pushed further back. Skirmishes and wars followed wherever the new settlers went. Some of our Founding Fathers fought and killed them. George Washington fought in wars against them. Andrew Jackson instituted the Indian Removal Plan whereby they were all driven west of the Mississippi. A large number were sent to Oklahoma - the Trail of Tears. Congress passed the Indian Reservation Act which placed them in reservations from which they could not leave without permission. They were slaughtered at the Sandy Creek Massacre in 1864 and later at Bighorn. In 1890 the US Army slaughtered them at Wounded Knee in South Dakota. Many Americans were awaiting the disappearance of the American Indian. Land was taken from them, they were decimated, their families were fragmented and sometimes they were forcefully converted to Christianity. Native Americans were actually prevented from practicing their own religion; this was a violation by the government of the of the First Amendment. Small wonder that they fought on the side of the British during the War of Independence! Unfortunately for them the British ceded their Indian territories to the victors of the War of Independence, the new country called the United States of America.

In 1607 the Jamestown Settlement in Virginia became the first English settlement in North America. It was named after King James I, and the site was chosen because it was inland, surrounded on three sides by water, which was deep and they could sail their ships in there and be protected. They found no Native Americans there and their chosen domain appeared to be defensible. They soon constructed a fort, and were protected by artillery. Despite the reasons for their choice diseases broke out, the drinking water was salty and caused illness amongst them, there was a drought and a famine, so much so that the Powhatan chief from nearby had to send in food to save their lives. After a while the chief was soured by the relationship with the settlers because he said they demanded too much. Many of the settlers died while the survivors clung to life by eating any animals they could get hold of and also some of their co-settlers who were unfortunate enough to have died. The colony was abandoned in 1619, but then it was reinforced by a ship from Bermuda which brought in more settlers with tobacco seeds – a means of starting a new enterprise. Africans were delivered to them in order to aid them in the hard-working tobacco business. Ten years of fighting with the Powhatans followed as a result of their infringement upon Powhatan land. There was even a civil war amongst the settlers who disagreed with the manner in which some of the other settlers were dealing with the natives.

The Pilgrims had been a group of Separatists in England who were seeking religious freedom from King James I. They were dissatisfied with the way in which the Church of England, to whom they belonged, had been practicing their religion. They left England and went to Amsterdam in Holland, later moving to Leyden. They were not doing too well economically, and so after some time they decided to go to the New World where they could live off the land and retain their English language and heritage and practice their religion in the manner which they thought was correct. In September 1620 – about thirteen years after the Jamestown Settlement - they set sail from Plymouth Harbor on the Mayflower (having returned to England) and arrived at a place which they called Plymouth Rock on Cape Cod. They had intended landing further south in the region of New York, but rough seas caused them to remain at the place where they had arrived; they chose discretion rather than valor. In the next few years more repressive religious policies by King James caused more separatists to leave England on small ships until in 1630 1,000 Puritans (they came from the same separatist movement as the Pilgrims) landed at Massachusetts Bay. The original settlers had a good relationship with the Native Americans when they first met them. They learnt much from them about growing fruits and vegetables, and celebrated their first Thanksgiving together. However, with the elapse of time and as the settlers took over more and more territory, tempers began to flare and little wars developed, interfering with the economy of the settlements and their relationships with the natives.

Native Americans loved the land, studied the birds and animals, grew their crops and then moved on to another place. They never owned any land and thought that the land belonged to everyone, and nobody should own any land. They were upset when they discovered that the White settlers wanted to own as much land as they could. If the White settlers were unable to occupy the land for any reason, they would buy it or fight for it – but the land must be theirs.

European settlements were devastating to Native Americans. With no immunity to the diseases of the White man they were unable to fight his diseases, such as smallpox and measles. They died by the thousands. While the Europeans took more of their land they were driven away from the burial places of their ancestors which were sacred to them, and they lost their identities. The French fur traders arrived, and apart from their financial ambitions they were trying very hard to convert them to Catholicism. Horses and guns employed by the settlers overpowered them and caused them to be easy fodder in most skirmishes and wars. European settlements were growing fast while the natives were being forcefully pushed back and into reservations. They resisted the White colonization but were forced to surrender. However, the introduction of farm animals – sheep, pigs and horses – from Europe proved a boon to them, and gave them work on their reservations. They, too, were proficient at horsemanship and marksmanship when they were able to get their hands on horses and guns.

Jean Jacques Rousseau, the French writer and philosopher at the time of the French Revolution, maintained that the Native Americans were people who had been totally free, freer than civilized Europeans. They had no masters other than nature and the weather. They had no police, no laws, no guns and no religion. When the White Man arrived freedom became a thing of the past.

During the American Revolution they fought on the side of the British, but at the end of the war they felt cheated when the British gave them and their territories to the Americans. They felt and looked like a defeated people. After the war the Americans needed farms and settlements so they grabbed or purchased whatever they could. George Washington had a civilizing plan for them. He asked people to treat them with justice, do commerce with them, civilize and improve them, and to those Americans who violate their rights he promised them punishment. Of course, like many of our Founding Fathers, he was a slave-owner.

The settlers' territory was expanding westward. In the nineteenth century there were battles between Native Americans and the settlers. Tecumseh was a Shawnee leader who really wanted peace with the White population, but he first gathered an army amongst a number of tribes and fought many battles against the Whites. There were battles at Little Bighorn and at Wounded Knee. At Little Bighorn in Montana the US 7th Cavalry suffered a major defeat which was partly countered at Wounded Knee in South Dakota in 1890 when 250 Native Americans were killed, including many women and children. Tecumseh fought on the side of the British in the War of 1812, but got killed in battle.

Following the War of Independence and towards the end of the 18th century the port of New Orleans was handling much of the overseas trade of the United States. France had controlled the area around the port, but she ceded it to Spain in 1762. However, it was returned to France in 1800. Napoleon was about to invade England, and was short of money considering the cost of all the wars in which the French were involved and the wars still to come in the future. New Orleans was far from Europe and thus difficult to manage so far away especially as the other French possession in the Western Hemisphere, Haiti, had just declared independence. Jefferson was dying to get New Orleans with its important port under United States control while Napoleon wanted to rid himself of such a heavy burden. So a deal was arranged. He sold Louisiana to the United States. It was far more than the state of Louisiana. It consisted of all land west of the Mississippi as far as the east side of the Rockies and from New Orleans to the Canadian border, constituting over 800,000 square miles. It was sold for fifteen million dollars or 18 dollars per square mile. The Louisiana Purchase included over a dozen states or parts of states, and it doubled the size of the United States. This, too, was land where Native Americans had been living for thousands of years.

The 19th century was a great time for the United States as far as territorial acquisitions are concerned. In 1819 Spain gave up Florida to the US. Spain was short of money and not able to handle policing and keeping control of the territory. There were runaway slaves coming in from the US South and Native Americans wandering in to their territory. Andrew Jackson was sent to invade Florida. Spain ceded the land to the US and in return the US recognized Spanish ownership of Texas.

Texas was a part of Mexico. Many US citizens went to live in Texas because the land was cheap. They brought their own slaves with them, even though Mexico did not sponsor slavery. Because of the slavery problem and because they did not like the laws instituted by Santa Anna, the Governor, they and many Mexicans living in Texas decided to fight for their independence. Santa Anna besieged them at the Alamo, but Sam Houston defeated Santa Anna at San Jacinto a short time later, thus bringing independence to Texas in 1837. Martin van Buren did not want Texas as a slave state, so he did not incorporate it into the US fearing that it would increase his problems. However, in 1845 Polk became the new President of the US. He was in favor of land expansion and heard the pleas of the Texans who wanted to join the United States. Mexico did not wish to see Texas as a part of the US. Polk asked Congress to declare war on Mexico and annexed Texas after a number of skirmishes at the border. Texas entered the union as a slave state.

Mexico and the US were at war from 1846 to 1848. Financially Mexico was almost bankrupt. Its ports were blockaded by American vessels, and she was unable to export or import goods, or benefit from taxation on goods. The Mexican Cession took place in 1848 and was followed by the Treaty of Guadalupe-Hidalgo in 1850. Mexico gave away more than 50% of its land mass. The Rio Grande was decided upon as the border and the US gained 520 million square miles of territory which included California, Nevada, Arizona, Utah, New Mexico and parts of Colorado, Oklahoma, Kansas and Wyoming. The entire area that Mexico ceded - the South-West United States - is known as the Mexican Cession. All people living in this area were granted US citizenship. The Gadsden Purchase of 1854 added another 290 square miles to Arizona and New Mexico. This, too, intensified the conflict of whether to allow slavery in the captured territories. The US also paid Mexico 15 million dollars plus the moneys claimed by Mexico from the citizens of Texas. Those Mexicans living in US-occupied Mexico were given the opportunity of becoming US citizens or moving to unoccupied areas of Mexico.

In the Northern states many people were not anxious to receive such a large parcel of territory which included California for fear of the impending problem of whether slavery would be allowed in these new states. As a matter of fact, this new problem of adding more slaves into the states was one of the causes leading to the Civil War.

With the discovery of gold in California the gold rush greatly increased the population, and the people of California voted against slavery. Three hundred thousand people arrived in the 1849 Gold Rush in order to seek their fortunes. They came by land and by sea. They came from within and from outside the land. Thousands of indigenous Native Americans were driven off their land or killed with impunity, their property trampled upon. The old American Dream of the Pilgrims - living off the land and practicing their religion without fear – now gave way to the desire of becoming rich quickly as a result of the new idol – gold.

The massive enlargement of the population and territorial acquisitions of the United States in the 19th century was the result of Manifest Destiny, the American dream at that time and a belief that was uppermost in the minds of many people. America, they said, was justified to expand throughout the Northern Hemisphere, and it was inevitable that they should bring the fruits of civilization, culture and Christianity to these backward lands. It was destined by God to spread capitalism and democracy even if some people suffered or died in the process. America felt that it was up to her to advance the lives of all the people on the continent. It was justifiable for her to remove Native Americans from where they lived and roamed, just as slavery was justifiable. The demands of an advancing civilization must not be blocked by minor matters! Development of the continent must continue. The Monroe Doctrine had demanded "Don't interfere with our march to the Pacific!"

In 1846 Oregon country was ceded by Britain to the US. The 49th parallel was recognized as the northern border while the entire Vancouver Island was ceded to Britain as a part of Canada. Together with the transfer of Oregon to the United States came the Native Americans who were living in that area. They were being handed to the US as subjects, whereas previously Native Americans had been either running away or being pushed back by the advancing giant – the United States. Now it seemed that there was nowhere left to run!

Before the Civil War John Brown, an abolitionist, together with a group of his men, attacked slave owners in Virginia, Kentucky and wherever and whenever they could. He said that speeches and sermons had been ineffective in freeing the slaves, and thus he created insurrections in order to aid their fight for liberty. He led many slaves across the Canadian border. However, he and his men were caught, and tried under laws of treason and conspiracy with slaves. John Brown ended up in a hangman's noose. Before he died, he said "The crimes of this country will not be purged away, but with blood."

The acquisition of the new territories introduced a big problem as far as slavery was concerned. The Missouri Compromise of 1820 had clearly stated that the southern border of Missouri was as far as slavery was permitted. In 1837 Texas entered the Union as a pro-slave state. The Mexican Cession left each new state to make its own decision. The Wilmot Proviso eliminated slavery from states gained from the Mexican War. It was approved by the House but did not pass in the Senate. It all sounded like one big mess. The northern states were in favor of the Wilmot Proviso because in the absence of slavery there would be more work available for Whites in the newly attained states. The Wilmot Proviso turned out to be a major cause of the Civil War.

The bloodiest war in American history broke out in 1861. It was a civil war with brother fighting and killing brother. It is commonly looked upon as a moral conflict concerning slavery, but it was probably more like a matter of political control and the economics of slavery. States Rights played a major part in the controversy. Did the federal government have the right to interfere in the slavery of individual states? The southern states said that it was their private concern. Southern states wanted to abolish the federal laws that they were not willing to support. The northern states were basically industrial while the southerners tended to be in the agricultural sphere and were the slave-owners. In fact, there were about four million African slaves. The labor in the North was performed mainly by new immigrants who later usually advanced in status in their own lives or in their children's lives. Matters were different in the case of slaves where they and their children remained slaves, as did their grandchildren in every succeeding generation, with no advancement for their offspring in sight.

Abraham Lincoln had been elected as President, but he got there without a single electoral college vote from the south. By now the southern states felt as though they were outside the political system. They spoke of secession. In 1861 southern soldiers surrounded Fort Sumter, a Federal military base in South Carolina, and asked the Federal troops to leave. When they refused to do so, they were fired upon, but finally the Federal troops surrendered. The Civil War had started. When the other southern states were asked by the Federal government to help put down the rebellion at Fort Sumter they refused. The war was a huge drain on the country not only in the loss of lives, but also in finances. By the time it ended more than 600,000 soldiers lost their lives. This was more than in any other war in which America has been involved. After the Proclamation of Emancipation which was issued in 1862 many runaway slaves joined the Northern army. After numerous battles the South under Robert E. Lee formally surrendered to Ulysses Grant at Appomattox court house in 1865, and the southern states that had seceded from the Union returned to it. Abraham Lincoln was assassinated soon after the end of the Civil War.

The Reconstruction Period then commenced. Andrew Johnson, a Democrat who followed Lincoln, started with a discriminatory system of regulations against the ex-slaves, but when the congressional Republicans took over matters improved and more rights were given to the freed slaves.

Yet the southerners tried to dampen the laws set in motion by the Federal government. They introduced what is known as Jim Crow Laws. They attempted to bypass Reconstruction by removing civil rights, enacting a poll tax in order to be able to vote, using separate records for Black people, separate water fountains in the parks, and other forms of discrimination. This continued until civil rights laws were introduced by Lyndon Johnson as late as 1965.

Scalawags were White Southerners who supported the Federal Reconstruction Program and co-operated with the Blacks. They were despised by the majority of Southerners for their attitudes which was considered to be disloyal. Carpet baggers were another group of Whites who were hated by the majority of Southern Whites. They were Northerners who arrived with one bag and a carpet (supposedly) to assist in Reconstruction efforts. Southerners said that they came to get rich while pretending to be helpful.

Alaska was purchased from Russia for 7 million dollars in 1867. The size of the territory was almost 660,000 square miles. The Russians had already penetrated as far as northern California, but they found that Alaska contained poor land and had a climate not conducive for growing foodstuffs. Only a few Russians had gone to live there. Besides, Russia was in need of money to help pay for the expensive Crimean War which had already been fought, so the money thus received appeared to be worthwhile to them. Since the departure of Russia it has been found that Alaska is a wealthy land with great riches in metals and ores.

In 1893 the monarchy in Hawaii was overthrown by a group of businessmen living there who did not like the way in which the country was being run. They sought aid from the United States to help them consolidate their victory and they wanted the US to eliminate the exorbitant sugar tariffs, but Grover Cleveland did not wish to annex these Pacific islands. Instead, he wanted to restore the Hawaiian Queen, but the coup members preferred Hawaii to remain as a Republic. In 1898 Hawaii became a part of the United States real estate when McKinley became president. By this time the Spanish-American War made Americans realize how valuable Pearl Harbor would be to the US as a naval base in the Pacific.

The Spanish-American War of 1898 was started on a pretext that the Spanish bombed the USS Maine, an American ship, in Havana harbor in Cuba. It was later declared that the fire on the ship was most likely started in the ship's kitchen and that Spain was not guilty. Nevertheless, the US went to war against Spain and gained Cuba (since then it has become independent), the Philippines (also free since then), Puerto Rica and Guam.

The twentieth century saw America's greatness come to the fore. It led the free world in two world wars, which might not have been won without her help. America saved democracy and freedom on both occasions. I have discussed these wars in the chapter called "Wars to End All Wars".

Earlier in the twentieth century the country went through a period known as the Roaring Twenties. It was a period of economic growth and prosperity. Art and culture made strides while Jazz music blossomed and spread throughout the world. The horse and cart were abandoned as a means of transportation while the automobile industry developed and thrived. Gadgets and electrical appliances were invented for the house, especially for the kitchen, which made living easier and less laborious. Telephones, radio, movies, and later, television developed, altering everyday living to a style such as it had never existed before. Women got rid of their Victorian garments and dressed differently. Then people took to the skies, flying to all corners of the earth on business, for pleasure and to see friends and family. America was on top of the world, and the world was shrinking.

It became a more exciting place to live in – until in 1929 there was a crash which could soon be felt everywhere.

Wall Street crashed! The market dropped and the country was in a Great Depression. Poverty reared its ugly head, people lost their jobs, many were unable to afford and supply enough food for the table to feed their families. Of those who did not lose their jobs they found that their income and salaries had decreased. Half the banks in the country failed in the face of people taking out large loans. Factories closed and farmers lost their lands and their homes because agriculture was struggling.

Why did the Great Depression arrive when everything was looking so good? Apparently with the Roaring Twenties people were spending a great deal more than they possessed and their social positions fell to lower levels. The government had set a high tax on imports, so there was little importing going on. The stock market crashed because its prices were over-valued while production was down and unemployment was up. At the same time there was a drought in Oklahoma. People were losing their jobs on their unproductive farms. Unemployment was rife, and the jobless farmhands were trying to find somewhere else in the country where they could make a living and survive. Ah, California! The President at the beginning of the Depression was Herbert Hoover. When it came to re-election he was defeated by Franklin D. Roosevelt. Roosevelt introduced the New Deal whereby he opened up many different programs in the country which introduced workers to numerous jobs and did much to relax the pressures that the Great Depression inflicted upon most Americans. The Depression did not come to an end until World War II began when many more jobs became available as a result of military needs and the expansion of the war industry.

Thus on these pages we have seen how a small colony on the Atlantic coast of North America, which commenced early in the seventeenth century grew to stretch across an entire continent as far as the Pacific coast-line and beyond within a time period of less than two hundred years. It was accomplished by fair means and foul. The Native American people suffered, as did the African-Americans and Latinos. Today the US has the third largest population amongst the countries of the world. It is the father of all democratic lands, the most powerful country, the wealthiest, the most advanced in the sciences and medicine. This all started with the

Jamestown colony and the landing of the Mayflower at Plymouth four hundred years ago.

All the land grabs of the nineteenth century on the North American continent would probably have been halted or at least argued by the United Nations and numerous governments and countless organizations in the present day. There were no such world bodies or organizations in previous centuries. The United States certainly has come a long way despite the fact that not all scholars would agree with some of the methods embarked upon in achieving those ends.

Apart from being a very large country the US does have a number of small dependencies – Puerto Rico, Guam, the Virgin Islands and some others. It is no longer trying to add to its Manifest Destiny of the nineteenth century. Our theme has been "Empires Come, Empires Go". America has not been considered to be an Empire. Even though it is a very large country, it is all under one roof, so to speak; fifty states - forty-eight of them contiguous – under one government. The US is the greatest democracy the world has ever known. The world regards America as a savior when it comes to attacks by tyrants and despots. Europe has been saved twice in the last century by the US. Every country hopes that, if they should be in trouble, the US will be there to aid them. It is a country that stands for justice, fairness and equality. But the US will have to be vigilant because of late there have been signs of some unscrupulous people in the American government who are disobeying the Constitution and attempting to tamper with the rights that have been fought for in the last two hundred and fifty years. Aiding and abetting them are people who are trying to divide the country into two poles, splitting the nation instead of unifying it. Their actions are anti-democratic. Their attempts are setting up chaos. America, beware of tyrants and egotists, dictators and racists, and wolves in sheep's clothing! Unity is strength!

CONQUISTADORS

———◆———

THE CONQUISTADORS WERE THE SPANISH and Portuguese explorers that sailed to the four corners of the earth and discovered land which helped to boost the size, strength, trade and finances of their countries, but there was also a desire to convert the heathens on the land to Christianity. Even before Columbus these Iberian sailors were able to travel long distances, hugging the shore-lines, but they could not safely enter the open seas. If they happened to be deep in the ocean with no land visible on the horizon they were lost as they knew not where they were nor where they were heading. In the early fifteenth century Prince Henry the Navigator, son of the King of Portugal, sent ships to sail the European and North African waters (he did not sail himself), but the ships did not go far from the shore-line for fear of the unknown and the hidden dangers of the high seas. Then came Abraham Zacuto.

Abraham Zacuto was a Jewish rabbi living in Salamanca, Spain. He was also an astronomer, and he modernized the astrolabe. When in 1492 the Jews were expelled from Spain, Zacuto moved to Portugal where he was given a high position in the King's court for his advances in astronomy. Vasco Da Gama sailed for the Orient from Portugal via the Cape of Good Hope to India with Zacuto's astrolabe, as did Columbus when he searched for the Orient by sailing west and landing in the West Indies. From this time the oceans were opened up and exploration developed rapidly. Once the Caribbean could easily be reached from Spain their sailors explored the islands of Hispaniola, Puerto Rico and Cuba. From there they were within easy reach of North, Central and South America.

In 1521 Ferdinand Magellan, who was Portuguese but sailed for Spain, became the first person to circum-navigate the world. He did not complete the voyage – he was killed by natives in the Philippines – but his crew finished it for him. They had been converting the natives to Christianity. While most accepted the new religion without any argument, the natives on one of the Philippine islands not desiring religious conversion went to war with them. One of the casualties was the murder of Magellan. Five ships and 270 men had set off originally on the expedition, but only one ship and about 20 men came home.

Who were these brave conquistadors who ventured into the unknown where no man had been before? They were men living a boring existence with little to do but who hungered for fame and adventure. What could be more exciting than joining a ship with an unknown destination and traveling into an unknown world? It was not unlike today's astronauts flying into space.

Hernan Cortes was such a person, born in Extremadura, Spain. Strangely, many of the Spanish conquistadors came from Extremadura. Balbao and De Soto came from there, and so did Pizarro, who was a cousin to Cortes. Cortes had an undistinguished childhood and early manhood, and was looking for an improvement in his life; so he went off to Hispaniola at the age of 19. He joined the forces that conquered Hispaniola, and then went to Cuba to fight in the take-over of the island. He settled there and got a job in the governor's office. He became a good friend of the governor, but it did not last long and their relationship became adversarial. He tried to organize an expedition going to the mainland, but the governor who, at first, recommended him for the voyage changed his mind and later intended to stop it. Cortes ignored the governor, and went ahead. When he arrived on the mainland of the American continent he made friendships with the local tribes. The governor of Cuba, no longer his friend, sent troops to arrest him but the friendships he had made on the mainland paid off as they helped to protect Cortes from his assailants.

He arrived on the American continent at the right time, because the Aztec Faith had promised that their god and creator was either coming back to earth or sending an emissary to aid them. Montezuma, the Aztec leader, was there to welcome and celebrate the arrival of Cortes, whom he thought must be their god and creator or, at least, his emissary. With such a welcome it was difficult for Cortes to fail. However, Montezuma soon realized that he had made a mistake. Cortes took him in as his prisoner, during which time Montezuma died. Cortes continued fighting whatever resistance was left and conquered the Aztecs, bringing a new country – Mexico – under the Spanish crown. King Charles made him governor of New Spain (Mexico).

There was a great deal of arguing and in-fighting within the Spanish officialdom in Hispaniola, Cuba and Mexico – and as a matter of fact, in most of the Spanish colonies. Cortes commented that he was having more trouble with his own people than with the Aztecs. Generally, the conquistadors were known to be cruel and ruthless, and to frequently commit atrocities and steal gold and precious metals. Often, if their Native American workers did not produce their gold quota their hands were cut off. The natives looked upon their conquerors as being evil. It is said that in the first century following the arrival of the White man the native population of the Americas was reduced by 90%. This was caused not only by conquistadors killing Native Americans but also by diseases brought in by the newcomers against which the natives were ill-equipped to resist.

While in Mexico Cortes took over Honduras as well, but on his return from Honduras he found that Ponce De Leon had been sent to investigate him. The authorities feared that he was becoming too powerful, and they did not trust him. He was fired from the governorship of New Spain. As a side-line he explored the California coast-line and Baja California. Then he decided to return to Spain in order to discuss the political on-goings and his own career with King Charles. While in Spain nothing came of his discussions but he was asked to join the forces that were being sent out to storm Algiers where the Corsairs were at that time. These were pirates under Barbarossa from the Ottoman Empire who were responsible for the attacks on Spanish ships in the Mediterranean. After this engagement he returned to Mexico for a short time, but finally ended up in Spain again where he died in Seville in 1547.

In 1810 after three hundred years as a Spanish colony Miguel Hidalgo, a Catholic priest who was also a Creole, started a movement which turned into a war demanding independence from Spain. During Napoleon's Peninsular Campaign many South American countries had already become encouraged and started talking of independence from Spain. Hidalgo was captured outside Mexico City and executed, but the struggle continued without him. A liberal government came into power in Spain at this time, and the new government wanted to help the freedom seekers. This made it easier for Mexico to declare independence from Spain in 1821. At the same time it put an end to slavery. Mexico was in dire straits. Texas, which was a part of Mexico and also where a large number of ex-Americans lived, broke away from Mexico in 1836. Remember the Alamo! The Texans failed in defending the Alamo against Santa Anna's forces, but gained independence by defeating him at San Jacinto a few months later.

The US invaded Mexico in 1846. This excursion ended with the Treaty of Guadaloupe-Hidalgo, following which the US took over Texas, California, New Mexico, Arizona, Utah, Colorado and Wyoming, including parts of Oklahoma and Kansas from Mexico. This territory constituted more than one-half of Mexico.

Then the Mexicans appointed a Caudillo (strong man) in the form of Santa Anna, who had recently been defeated by the Texans. There was so much chaos in the country that Santa Anna was soon overthrown. He was replaced by Benito Juarez, a liberal. At this time French, Spanish and British troops landed in Mexico for the purpose of collecting a debt owed to them, but which Juarez decided not to re-pay because of the bad economic situation through which they were passing. Napoleon III had other ideas, too, as he saw how weak and poor Mexico was. He thought it might be a good plan to extend his French Empire to include Mexico. The British and Spanish forces withdrew when they realized Napoleon III's plans. Juarez and his government evacuated the capital and moved away. Mexican conservatives decided that they would like to have a monarchy, and so Napoleon III gave them one by installing Maximilian I, a Habsburg. By this time the American Civil War was over, and Abe Lincoln was not happy to see an extension of the French monarchy at his doorstep. In 1867 Napoleon III decided to withdraw rather than go to war with the US. Maximilian was overthrown, caught and executed. Juarez returned as Caudillo.

Let us move on to some other conquistadors. Francisco Pizarro also came from Extremadura; he was a distant cousin of Cortes. He was born in Trujillo in about 1471, illegitimate and a part of a poor family. He had little or no education, but wanted some adventure in his life. So he went to South America, and accompanying Vasco Nunez Balboa, they made the first crossing by Europeans of the Isthmus of Panama, and were the first Europeans to view the Pacific Ocean from the American continent – not a bad beginning for a poor young man with a boring existence! Later he was made mayor of Panama City. The new governor of Panama (Davilla) who succeeded Balboa did not trust him (Balboa) so he asked Pizarro to arrest Balboa – the man who took him across Panama. He obeyed and had Balboa arrested, and Davilla had Balboa executed.

Pizarro joined two expeditions to conquer Peru, but both failed. He returned to Spain and showed King Charles some of the gold and riches that they had brought back from their Peruvian excursions. With pressure from Pizarro and the sight of all those jewels Charles gave Pizarro permission to undertake the third expedition into Peru. With a few hundred men Pizarro set forth to invade Peru. Once there he was invited by the Inca emperor to his palace. When Pizarro made demands upon the emperor he refused his demands, reasoning that he had an army of fifty thousand men as compared to Pizarro's two hundred. Nevertheless, a fight ensued and the emperor was taken hostage. A ransom was asked for, and the emperor immediately produced the gold and silver that Pizarro had demanded. Pizarro was still not completely satisfied, and had the emperor executed. In 1531 Pizarro and his men completed the conquering of Peru once they took over Cuzco, the capital. When Charles heard of the execution of the Inca emperor he was displeased.

Pizarro went on and founded the city of Lima, where he decided that he would like to live. After the final battle of the conquest of Peru, Almagro, one of the higher standing officers under Pizarro, had a dispute with him about certain areas of governance. This dispute had not been settled, when one day while Pizarro was at home in Lima, about twenty men sent by Almagro entered his home and assassinated him.

Peru was always loyal to Spain. Even while South American countries fought for independence Peru for many years did not budge. The Viceroyalty of Peru was the largest Spanish colony in the world. It included Bolivia and Argentina. If a new colony was founded in South America it usually became a part of Peru.

Amerigo Vespucci was an Italian from Florence, but he was sent to Spain by the Medici family for whom he worked. He was interested in cartography and exploration, and joined expeditions to the New World, first sailing for Spain and later sailing for Portugal. Not all that has been written about Vespucci's voyages are considered to be authentic, but his trip to Rio de Janeiro where he was the first white man to arrive is considered as true. He also went south to Patagonia and then returned. Of course, the South American continent was named after him. Soon the North American continent also took on his name. While under the Portuguese command he was with Goncaio Coelho when they came across a river in 1502 which they named Rio de la Plata (River of Silver). The capitals of both Argentina and Uruguay are on the Rio de la Plata, but it was not until 1516 that Juan de Solis established settlements there.

Amongst the settlers that subsequently arrived were many Spanish and Portuguese Jews who had been exiled by the Spanish Inquisition and then went to live in Portugal, only to be exiled again by the Portuguese Inquisition some years later. Many Jews went to live in Brazil. Many settlers came to Argentina from Peru. They found it to be good cattle and farming country. At that stage there was no evidence of gold or silver in the earth even though the name of the country was Argentina which comes from the Latin word 'argentum', meaning silver. Apparently, the mountains had a silvery appearance at certain times of the day, hence the name.

When Napoleon finally defeated the Spanish and Portuguese in the Peninsular War King Joao, his family and entourage fled to Brazil (1808) and took command of the Portuguese Empire from there. In 1821 the King returned to Lisbon in order to quell a disturbance. Napoleon was long gone, but there was rioting by the local populace in Lisbon. He left his son, Don Pedro, in charge of Brazil. A year later, Don Pedro declared independence from Portugal – and his father. In 1888 slavery was abolished in Brazil, and the ex-slaves united with the military to overthrow the monarchy, leaving Brazil as an independent republic.

Chile had been a part of the Incan Empire when the conquistadors arrived. After taking over Peru Pizarro sent Pedro de Valdivia and his men from Peru to conquer Chile in 1540. Magellan had already been there in the early sixteenth century while on his circum-navigation of the world, but he had only passed through and made no claim on the land. De Valdivia, like many conquistadors, was also born in Extremadura, so he called the country he conquered Nueva Extremadura. In 1541 he founded Santiago and became its first governor. He refused to accept any titles or salary until Pizarro died because he felt that acceptance would be disloyalty to Pizarro. The first years after the conquest were hard because of the poverty the Spanish settlers endured as well as the rebellions and burnings by the natives. The local Amerindians lacked the discipline of labor, so it was difficult to get much accomplished. When de Valdivia's men tried to take over the southern long strip of Chile the climate was too cold for them and they returned home as they did not possess the incentive to continue.

Most of the settlers in Chile came down from Peru. Some came down the east coast of South America, which was easier and better known than the Chilean coast, although the Chilean coast had been used by pirates and British explorers to try to penetrate its shores – including Sir Frances Drake – but none succeeded.

De Valdivia died during one of the internal rebellions in 1553. Chile declared independence from Spain in 1818 when Jose San Martin defeated the royalist forces.

Simon Bolivar was born in Caracas, Venezuela in 1783. Venezuela was a Spanish colony in the Viceroyalty of New Granada, which was the northern portion of South America consisting of Colombia, Panama, Ecuador and Venezuela. He was born to a wealthy family of Basque descent. Both his parents died while he was very young, and so he was brought up by Hipolita, one of the slaves who had tended to the family, and he remained very close to her. He received a fine education from excellent tutors. One of his teachers, Don Simon Rodriguez, was forced to flee the country because he had been preaching freedom and spreading anti-government propaganda. Bolivar went to Spain to further his education. He visited France where he witnessed Napoleon Bonaparte at the Notre Dame Cathedral grabbing the crown out of the hands of the Pope and crowning himself as Emperor.

When Bolivar returned to Venezuela he freed all his own slaves; they had been left over by his family. He was an abolitionist fifty years before Lincoln freed the slaves in the US. He was given a military command, and he was in the army when Venezuela became the first South American country to gain independence from Spain. He joined the revolutionaries. But there was too much in-fighting amongst the generals and an earthquake added to the chaos, so Spain had little difficulty in re-claiming the country. Fighting continued against Spain, but Bolivar and the local inhabitants were unable to defeat them, even with the aid of British, Haitian and other troops. Bolivar went to Lima, Peru in 1821 and fought the Spanish from there. He freed the northern part of Peru, which was called Bolivia. He wrote the constitution and was made president of Bolivia. Soon after that he was made president of Colombia. In 1824 he was declared dictator of Peru. Only as a part of Bolivar's all-out campaign in Nueva Granada did Venezuela finally receive its freedom from Spain. This occurred in 1821 under the leadership of Bolivar, after many years of intermittent fighting.

Then he envisaged a federation of South America similar to the United States, but he was resigned to the fact that the South Americans were a different people, less obedient and would not be easily led. There was much fighting amongst the leaders, and Bolivar decided to become a dictator of Peru, Bolivia, Colombia and Venezuela on a temporary basis until the fighting amongst his people would stop. There followed an assassination attempt on his life, so he retired. He died in 1830, supposedly of tuberculosis, but at autopsy arsenic was found in his body. Was this foul play? Arsenic was frequently found in medication in those days. The cause of death remains inconclusive.

Jose de San Martin who was born in Argentina in 1778 was another Spanish American freedom fighter. He fought with Bolivar to help free Chile and Peru. He went to Malaga, Spain for study, but after a while he found himself fighting with the Spanish forces in the Peninsular War against Napoleon. Napoleon named his brother to be in charge of Spain while he went on his way to conquer what was still left unconquered in Europe. While the Peninsular War was being waged and Spain was deeply involved in defending herself the Spanish American colonies became more forthright about demanding independence.

When San Martin returned to South America he was supposed to join the Spanish army to protect the Spanish Empire from dissidents. However, he soon changed his mind, and became an independence fighter. He was responsible for gaining independence for Argentina by defeating the royalist forces in 1818. Having become a hero in Argentina he decided that the liberation of Peru was the key to independence of Spanish America. He crossed the Andes with about 5,000 men and with little difficulty he liberated Chile. From there he formed a Chilean Navy so that he could sail his men to Peru.

At that time Bolivar was also busy conquering the northern portion of Peru. They fought together and liberated Peru and the rest of the

Viceroyalty. Bolivar and San Martin met at Guayaquil. Both were ambitious men. San Martin wanted to invite a monarch from Europe to lead the liberated territories because he felt that the South American people were too poor and insufficiently educated to be ready for democracy and self-rule. On the other hand, Bolivar wished for a local leader - meaning himself – to take complete charge. Not much is known as to what had ensued at their meeting in Guayaquil, but the outcome was that San Martin retired from the army and left South America in 1824. He went to live in France. Bolivar finished what San Martin had commenced.

Spain and Portugal opened up South and Central America, but their Empires have fallen. All that they left to the New World are their languages and their culture which have been diluted by the languages and culture of the indigenous population that have lived there for many thousands of years before the Europeans came to conquer them. The instinct for the desire for freedom in South America, as it is everywhere, was so strong that it continued to burn, no matter the odds, until victory was achieved. The conquistadors introduced civilization into the New World. Having done their job they were no longer needed.

Spain and Portugal did not limit their explorations and conquests to South America. The original premise was to find a route to the East. I am not sure if the Spanish and Portuguese explorers who went to Asia were referred to as conquistadors (as they were referred to in South America), but they played a similar, but lesser role, as explorers adding some territorial acquisitions to their homeland and spreading Christianity to the natives. A sea route around the southern tip of Africa was deemed necessary as the Muslims had spread into North Africa, the Middle East and south Asia, making land travel extremely dangerous. Obviously, there was no sea route from the Mediterranean as the Suez Canal had not been built yet.

Bartholomew Diaz was a Portuguese explorer. In 1488 he was the first European to set foot in South Africa after sailing through treacherous seas as he came around the Cape. He called it the Cape of Storms because of the dangerous currents set up by the Indian and Atlantic Oceans meeting with the wild Antarctic, but King Joao II later changed the name to the Cape of Good Hope, a more optimistic tone. Diaz went up the east coast of South Africa, as far as the mouth of the Fish River. At a later date, in 1500, he accompanied Alvares Cabral on his expedition to Brazil, but once having arrived there he and his ships re-crossed the Atlantic and went south again to South Africa. There, unfortunately, they came upon a cyclone and they all drowned in very rough seas. Perhaps the first name, the Cape of Storms, should have been a warning.

Ten years after Diaz's first trip around Africa Vasco da Gama, also a Portuguese navigator, followed in his footsteps. In 1498 he brought fame to his native land by being the first explorer to reach India via the long sea trip around the southern tip of Africa. He rounded the Cape of Good Hope and went up the east coast of Africa, stopping at Mozambique and Mombasa. The stops he took in East Africa were not always friendly and pleasant, as he had a number of skirmishes with Muslims in those areas, and left hastily before matters could grow worse. At Malindi he met an Indian seaman who guided him as he crossed the Indian Ocean. When he arrived in Calicut (also known as Kerala) in the southern corner of India he was not only the first European to get there across the oceans, but it was also the longest sea voyage ever undertaken.

He gave the Indian chief of Calicut gifts which he said had come from King Manuel of Portugal, but the chief was unimpressed, believing that he deserved more valuable presents than that after such a long voyage. He asked da Gama to pay custom charges for docking. In order to avert further contention da Gama set sail for home. Crossing the Indian Ocean from Calicut through storm-tossed and dangerous seas, he and his men fought their way through monsoons. It took them four months as compared to little over a month on their way across the Indian Ocean to get to Calicut. By the time they reached Malindi he had lost half his crew and had to scuttle some ships, leaving him only two. When he arrived back in Portugal he received many honors from the king for his efforts. He failed to bring back any trade agreements – all he brought home were some spices.

He made further trips to India. He and his men attacked ships in the Indian Ocean carrying Muslims on the way to the haj in Mecca. He robbed their ships and killed their passengers; his men performed acts of piracy and he had fights and skirmishes in India. But he made India realize that Portugal was a force to contend with, and this time he introduced a trade deal with India. Goa became a Portuguese colony in India. Mozambique, on the east coast of Africa, was also adopted into the Portuguese Empire, as was Angola on the west coast of Africa at a later date.

Diaz and da Gama, two Portuguese sailors and their men, with hearts of steel, displayed great courage to venture into uncharted oceans and unknown lands on the other side of the world. These two men, especially Da Gama who opened up the Orient for us and introduced trade with Europe, helped to make the world more connected and less mysterious. Yet Spain and Portugal, discoverers of continents, built Empires which no longer exist. We are the benefactors of their dreams and courage.

ISLAM

―――◇――――

I T IS STRANGE THAT ONE of the largest religions in the world, Islam, was born in a desert. It was conceived by a camel herder, and in a short space of time it spread in all directions capturing the minds and souls of the new believers. It spread like wild-fire, and today there are 1.6 billion adherents throughout the world. Mohammed was a human being, an ordinary man. He never claimed to be the son of God or possess any extra-terrestrial qualities like Jesus; nor was he born out of riches, like Buddha. His father was an Arab. Mohammed was born in Mecca, Arabia in 570 A.D. of ordinary parents. His mother died when he was about six years old, and he was brought up by his grandfather, and later, an uncle who never became a Muslim. He married his aunt who was one of the twelve wives he had during his life-time. He spent much time in the desert taking care of his aunt's camels. He said that he went to a certain cave in the desert every day, and there, Archangel Gabriel met him and spoke to him about God. From the information given to him by Gabriel he wrote the Quran, which is the Holy Bible of Islam. There are many characters from the Old Testament featured in the Quran, but it is unlikely that he ever read of them in the Bible as he probably spoke no Hebrew or Greek which were the only two languages at that time in which the Bible existed.

For those of us that are not very sure about believing whether a Holy man, Gabriel, who lived thousands of years before Mohammed was able to really converse with him, let me remind you that at that time there were many Jews living in Mecca and Medina, and there were many Jewish traders and travelers passing through on the Silk Road. They might have been a reliable source of information for Mohammed, especially when you understand that there are so many similarities between the Jewish and Islamic religions. In fact, they were more similar before Mohammed became incensed with the Jews, and removed certain rituals in order to punish them.

This is not the first time that Archangel Gabriel supposedly came out from his grave and gave advice to the living. He spoke to Daniel, interpreting his dream for him and he spoke to Mary, the mother of Jesus, informing her that the father of her child was not her husband Joseph, but the Holy Spirit.

Once he had formulated his newly found religion Mohammed had trouble in converting the people of Mecca to Islam. The idea of only one God did not appeal to most of the people who preferred the idea of multiple gods. The Jews living in Arabia were the only monotheistic people at that time. Mohammed did not consider Christians as monotheists, as they prayed to many; they prayed to God and to Jesus, and Mary and the Holy Ghost and sometimes to their saints. There was a fair amount of rioting following his attempts at converting the people of Mecca to Islam, and some of his followers fled to Abyssinia, where Christianity was rife and where Jews, too, had been arriving. Many of these followers returned to Mecca with information about Christianity and Judaism, which added to Mohammed's knowledge about these religions.

Having been unsuccessful in gaining converts in Mecca, he and his followers moved to Medina, where more people were receptive to him and rallied to his Islamic call. The migration to Medina in 622 is known as the Hejira – the date of the commencement of the Islamic calendar. There were wealthy Jews living in Medina. They were influential, and helped the economy by selling and exporting dates. Mohammed approached the Jews of Medina and asked them to convert to Islam considering that the two religions were so similar. It would have been a feather in his cap if the Jews of Medina had en masse converted to Islam. There was one major problem. In 333 B.C. the rabbis had decided that the era of prophecies was over. There will be no more prophets, said the wise men. Therefore, Christ had been unacceptable to the Jews, and now Mohammed, too, fell into the same category. The Jews refused to be converted. Mohammed was afraid that the Jews and non-believers would unite and go to war against him. He attacked them and killed 800 Jews. He took away their homes, their vineyards, equipment and methods they used for earning a living.

He sold their women and children into slavery. In the Quran, Sura 33 says "God defeated the Jews".

Abraham, Mohammed said, was a Muslim - Ebrahim. He built the Kaaba in Mecca with his son, Ishmael. The Kaaba had been a rock-like structure in existence seemingly forever where pagans came to pray to their gods. Mohammed declared it to be the first house of worship for the Muslims, and is now a visiting site for all those making pilgrimage to Mecca. Notice that in the Hebrew Bible Ishmael, the first son of Abraham, and Hagar who was his wife Sarah's handmaiden, are both sent off into the desert and are not heard of again, but here Mohammed has found a role for Ishmael. Isaac, a Jewish patriarch and the son of Abraham and Sarah and half-brother to Ishmael, is not recognized by Mohammed and not even mentioned by him.

At first Mohammed had said that Muslims would face Jerusalem during prayer. After the Jewish War he announced that they would face Mecca, and not Jerusalem, during prayer. Instead of fasting on one day per year as the Jews did – and Mohammed had proclaimed the same for his people - he changed his mind and said that they would now fast for the whole month of Ramadan from sunrise to sunset. Instead of praying three times per day like the Jews did, he said that was being changed to five times per day. Circumcisions were determined to be acceptable but not mandatory. God's laws remained, but man-made laws from the Bible were not to be observed. After-life, Paradise and angels had been discussed by Jews in the early days, but later were omitted from religious topics. Jews concentrated instead on the living. However, to Muslims after-life is an important part of their religion.

Distancing Islam from Judaism became Mohammed's goal. He accused the Jews of having killed their Prophets, as did Paul and Matthew. He loved their religion – that is why he originally made Islam as close to Judaism as was possible, and only changed much of it for revenge when the Jews did not join him. He accused the Jews of having altered God's words. He said that if you do not follow God then you must be a follower of Satan. Because of their diminished status Jews (and Christians) would have to pay protection money, known as dhimmi in Muslim lands. It was a tax to remind them of their subservience to Islam, and it was to be paid with humility while they would be treated with disdain while paying the dhimmi. He also said that the Jews were no longer God's Chosen People because they had continued to produce idols and golden calves, and that was also the reason for them not having a home and being spread throughout the world. Now the Muslims were God's Chosen People.

Islam became a religion that was easy for non-Muslims to join. One did not require an imam or holy person to convert you. There was no course or examination to succeed in, and once a Muslim everybody was equal, whether you were a king or a beggar. Circumcision – painful for adults - was not mandatory!

There are five pillars of Islam to which every Muslim must adhere. There is no god, but Allah, and Mohammed is his messenger. Muslims pray facing Mecca five times per day – dawn, noon, afternoon, sunset and after dark. Every person must give alms to the poor. Fasting occurs during the month of Ramadan from sunrise to sunset. Every Muslim must attempt to make at least one pilgrimage (haj) to Mecca in a lifetime.

Islam spread with the Arab trade which was moving on along the Silk Road, reaching Central Asia as far as India and Afghanistan. The Arabs were also good sailors, and so Islam spread into North Africa along with their North African trade. In a short time there were Muslims in Mali and as far down as Somalia, Mombasa, Dar-Es-Salaam and Zanzibar because Arabs were sailing south on the Indian Ocean. There was also a migratory process of Arabs leaving the Arabian Peninsula, because the land was hot and dry, infertile and unproductive. People wanted to get out of the desert. They did so, taking their trade together with their new found religion with them. Animists and polytheists turned to Islam, as some Jews and Christians also did. The Muslims decided that conversion should not be actively sought as long as there was subordination to Islam amongst the ambient population. Too many converts would dilute the economy and put an end to the dhimmi, which had helped to swell the coffers. Conversions would diminish the amount of dhimmi. However, this soon changed and became a matter of 'Allah or the sword' and mass conversions were forced and increased in large numbers. The growth of Islam weakened the status of Jews and Christians, and strengthened the power of Islam. The Muslim population increased faster than in other religious groups as each person was permitted to have four wives as well as a number of concubines. The Arabic language and writing and the use of Arabic numerals spread, as did

Arabic customs while schools and mosques were built wherever the Arab migrants settled. Some of the most beautiful mosques were built during that time. A mosque is translated as a "place for bowing".

Divisions occur in Islam. The most notable one results from changes that took place after the death of Mohammed in the first half of the 7th century. It was expected that after his death his place would be taken by his son-in-law, Ali, whom he had chosen as a successor. Instead the elders chose Abu Bakr, a very fine teacher and father of Aisha, the first wife of Mohammed. He was Caliph for a short time, and following his death two other Caliphs were chosen while Ali was still overlooked. However, Ali became the fourth Caliph. He was a peaceful man and did not wish to go to war with other Muslims to right the wrongs of the past. He was forced into a battle, which he won, but was assassinated. After Ali's death his son Hussein was invited to become a leader of a group of Shia in Iraq, but when he arrived he and his small group were attacked by the Caliph Yazid at Karbala. Hussein was killed. The anniversary of this event acts as a day of remembrance of the martyrdom of Hussein, and on that day every year, as a sign of sympathy for the events at Karbala many Shia will wound or torture themselves. Those who favored and supported the choice of Abu Bakr as Caliph are known as Sunni, and they constitute at least 80% of the world's Muslims. Those who believe that Ali was incorrectly overlooked are Shia, and most of them live in Iran and Iraq. This division has been responsible for much blood-shed through the centuries until this day.

While Europe was struggling through the Dark Ages Islam was thriving. The culture of the world was localized mainly in Islamic countries. Science, art and philosophy had found a new home. Thanks to Islam, European art and culture was preserved by Muslims, and therefore still exist today. They saved European literature, art and whatever they could, restored that which was damaged and translated manuscripts. If not for these efforts much would have been lost.

The Persians in the Islamic Empire did not have a good relationship with the Arabs. Firstly, the Persians are mostly Shia and the majority of Arabs are Sunni. Persia had been a large and powerful Empire since Biblical times. Their religion was Zoroastrianism until Islam arrived. The Persians looked upon the Arabs as an impoverished desert people. The conquest of Persia started in 637 and ended in 651 when the majority of Persians became Muslims. This was also the end of Zoroastrianism and the Sasanian Empire. All was not lost; the arts and culture and developments achieved in the Persian civilization were retained. The Arabs were delighted to absorb the fruits of Persian successes of the past and to be able to participate in them. The new Saphavid dynasty of Persia made Shia Islam the national religion. There were still Jews, Christians and some Zoroastrians allowed to live there, but the Bahai faith, regarded as apostates, was not acceptable – they were forced to convert or leave the country. Persia was Islamized, but not Arabized while the Arabs had much to gain from their latest acquisition.

In fact, it was the Persianized form of Islam that was exported to the Ottoman Empire, India, and Azerbaijan. The greatest philosophers, writers, poets and artists were Persian. Most of the Shia in the world are referred to as Twelvers. Apparently there were twelve Caliphs from the time that Ali became Caliph, who were in the family of Mohammed. The twelfth was a little boy who was hidden, and it is believed, never died. He, we are told, will become the Mahdi (Messiah) when the right time occurs, and will reign over all Islam.

The Umayyads were the first Muslim dynasty after the passing of Mohammed. They took over in 661, and followed the first four caliphs. They ruled from Damascus. The Umayyads originally came from Mecca and resisted Mohammed's introduction of Islam to them, which sent him off to Medina. Later they embraced Islam and became staunch supporters of the religion. The Umayyads spread Islam through the Middle East and North Africa. They even conquered the Iberian Peninsula, which they called Al-Andalus. They were eventually overthrown by the Abbasids who took over all their territory except Al-Andalus which they held on to until 1492. They were the ones who were responsible for the Golden Age in Spain when they introduced philosophers and poets, and encouraged the development of the arts and sciences. Spain and Portugal had a majority of Christians living there; there was also a large population of Jews. Non-Muslims were allowed to practice their religions unimpeded. After all, they worshipped the same God. They had to pay taxes for not being Muslims, and also were prevented from holding certain elevated positions.

The Abbasid dynasty that defeated the Umayyads after a civil war ruled from Baghdad. They lasted as a dynasty until 1258 when they were conquered by the Mongols. The Abbasids resulted from the offspring of Mohammed's uncle, Abbas, who was the third Caliph. There was a strong Persian influence in the Abbasid Caliphate as Baghdad was in Mesopotamia, which was part of the Persian Empire. The Persians were tired of being ruled by Arabs, whom they did not respect during the entire Umayyad years. Towards the end of their dynasty the Abbasid Caliphate weakened and began to splinter into fragmented territories, such as the Ismaeli Caliphate in Egypt and a Sasanian Empire in Persia. Then the Mongols came and laid waste to the land. Years later the Ottoman Empire took over where the Abbasids left off and resurrected whatever they could. Constantinople became the center of the Islamic world.

Other offshoots of the Islamic religion exist apart from Umayyads and Abbasids. There are the Sufis who added mysticism to their faith. They aim for a personal experience with God and shun materialism. Amongst the Sufis are the Whirling Dervishes who whirl around in circles while they pray. The Salafis are puritanical Islamists. Salafi means 'predecessor', and that is where they aim to be – they wish to live the lives of their forefathers.

In Saudi Arabia we have the Wahhabis who desire to return to the Islam of the early days under the Caliphate. They are fundamentalists and reject modern influences. In Saudi Arabia churches and synagogues will not be found. Only one religion may be practiced there, and that is Islam. No alcohol can be bought or served there. They do not wish to have foreigners or foreign influence in their country. They have built madrassahs throughout their land and all over the Middle East where the fundamentalist form of Islam is taught. Osama Bin Laden and many other extremists are alumni of the madrassahs. They believe in martyrdom, rewards in Heaven and eternal bliss.

There are the Alawites of Syria. Syria is ruled by the Alawites who are only 10% of their population. The Alawites are Shia Muslims but they have some Christianity added to their rituals, which causes other Muslims to believe that they are not true Muslims. They follow the rituals of Christmas and they practice the sacrament of flesh and blood. They also have a Trinity to whom they pray. It consists of Mohammed, Ali and Saliman (a Persian).

Historically, the Arabs lived for their families, clans and Allah.

Subsequently, after World War I many of their lands were taken over by European powers. Then, nationalism was introduced because it was intolerable for them to have a foreign power taking control of an Islamic country. They had to get the foreign powers out of their countries. Thus was born the Muslim Brotherhood and other such groups. The Quran discusses Jihad, or Holy War. It states that it is lawful to go to war against rebels, bandits, infidels, those who reject Allah, and those who do not believe in Allah and are invading your land.

The Crusaders took Jerusalem from the Muslims in 1099. Almost a hundred years later Saladin, a Kurd, re-captured Jerusalem (Jews were fighting on his side) after a prolonged siege, and drove the Crusaders out. He then invited the Jews to return. He was considered as a model Muslim commander by Christians and Jews.

When the Umayyads conquered Spain the Jews of Spain ran out to meet them and welcomed them since they had suffered under Catholic rule for many years. They thrived in Spain under the Muslims, despite the dhimmi and the closure of certain jobs to them. They held some high positions in the administration. When the Umayyads went off to France on an attempt to conquer the land – they were driven back by Charles Martell at the gates of Paris – they left the Jews to take care of Spain while they were at war. The Golden Age of Islam was also a Golden Age for the Jews in Spain at that time. Gradually over the years the Catholics pushed the Muslims further south until they were bottled up in Cordoba and its environs. Finally in 1492 the Muslims were ejected from Spain.

Two other events occurred in the same year. Christopher Columbus set out on his trip to discover the New World and the Jews were expelled from Spain by Ferdinand and Isabella The choice for the Jews was Christianity or exile. Most chose exile. The Sultan of the Ottoman Empire, the inheritors of Islam, invited all Jews who wished to come to Turkey and provided a free passage in ships which he sent to Spain for the purpose of picking them up. Jews lived in the Ottoman Empire comfortably and peacefully for many centuries.

During the twentieth century European colonialism started to grow. This was the time when the Ottoman Empire was weakening, finding its territories too far apart and difficult to manage while in-fighting among its leaders did little to improve the situation. European countries began nibbling at the outlying regions of the Ottoman Empire. Britain and France interfered in Egypt, and built and managed the Suez Canal without any hindrance from the Ottoman landlords. The British also interested themselves in Sudan. France made excursions into Algeria, Tunisia and Morocco – again, little or no Ottoman interference. In 1870 at the Treaty of Berlin European countries decided to make a scramble for countries in Africa. When World War I took place Lawrence of Arabia fought with the Arabs against the Ottomans, and after the war Britain awarded the Arabian ruler by giving his son Abdullah the Kingdom of Trans-Jordan and the other son Faisal the leadership of Iraq, but both countries were added to the British Empire. We have here examples of foreign powers on Muslim soil - the British in Iraq, Trans-Jordan and Egypt and the French in Syria. These were some of the causes of nationalism developing in Middle Eastern lands. Until then the Muslim male was protective of family, clan and Allah. Nationalism had not been in the forefront of his mind. Now his love for family and clan was turning towards nationalism and a desire to drive out the foreign powers.

In 1928 the Muslim Brotherhood was formed in Egypt. It was a strongly nationalistic organization with a religious background and influenced by the Wahhabis and their madrassahs. It spread to the other Middle Eastern Muslim lands. In Iraq and Syria it was called the Baath Party. In years to come Anwar Sadat, the head of State in Egypt, will be assassinated by a member of the Muslim Brotherhood for making peace with Israel.

In 1980 Iran and Iraq went to war against each other. The Baath Party in Iraq supported Saddam Hussein of Iraq whereas the Baath Party of Syria supported Iran and fought against the Baath Party of Iraq. This was because Saddam Hussein was Sunni (even though most of Iraq was Shiite) while Iran and Syria are Shiite. It appears as though blood is thicker than water. One of the causes for the war, apart from the growing hatred of Shia vs. Sunni, was a fight over the ownership of the Shat-al-Arab waterway where the Tigris and the Euphrates Rivers come together at the border between the two countries. The war lasted eight years, was responsible for over a half million deaths, and ended in a draw.

The formation of ISIS, or the Islamic State of Iraq and Syria, considered as a terrorist organization by the European Union and the United States, was also influenced by Wahhabi fundamentalism and the madrassahs. Strangely, even though Wahhabism helped to spore ISIS, the Saudis look upon them as enemies. ISIS wishes to set up a Caliphate as in the days after the death of Mohammed, but the Saudis wish to be the leaders of the Muslim world and do not want to have the competition which they receive from ISIS. Also, they do not wish to be associated with a terrorist group and have their name fouled. Strange as it seems, the teacher (the Saudis) looks upon the student (ISIS) as an enemy.

During World War II the Western Allies did not want the Middle East to fall into the hands of the Germans. It would have given the Germans great strength if they had controlled the Mediterranean and North Africa. Also, Winston Churchill was of the opinion that a Second Front should soon be opened up with an invasion of Italy from the Mediterranean. In the meantime British forces had to fight the Germans under Rommel in Egypt and Libya. Libya was an Italian possession, but Italian military forces were considered to be ineffectual by the Germans. So, Germany was forced to come to the rescue of the Italian forces, as so frequently occurred during World War II. When the Americans entered the war they sent troops to North Africa where they battled against the Germans and Vichy France. Vichy France (southern France, French colonies in North Africa and the French navy) was really under German control, but administered by France under Marshall Petain in order to lighten the Nazi burden.

British forces invaded Iran in order to create a channel for sending supplies to the Soviet Union through the Persian Gulf. The oil wells of Iran should not fall into the hands of the Germans. The Shah of Persia was pro-German so he was forced to resign. Britain also invaded Syria and Lebanon. The Middle East was now in the hands of the Allies.

After World War II Britain and France were exhausted and weakened. Without much resistance they allowed the Arab States to gain their independence. Oil and the Israel-Palestinian conflict became dominant features of post- World War II events in the Middle East. Western style democracy was attempted by some Arab states but they usually turned into dictatorial tyrannies as in the cases of the Assads in Syria, Nasser in Egypt and Saddam Hussein in Iraq. Nationalism grew and the young people looked upon Islam as backward. When it appeared possible that the United Nations General Assembly might vote in favor of giving a portion of Palestine to the Jews as a National Home the Pan-Arabism movement became anti-Israel and sought Soviet help as they turned away from the Western powers who, they said, had not fought hard enough to protect them.

When, in 1948 the United Nations General Assembly voted in favor of dividing Palestine into a Jewish and Palestinian state a large number of Arab states, including Egypt, Syria, Jordan and Iraq, attacked Israel from all sides. Israel protected herself and came out victorious in the Six Day War. Subsequent Israel-Arab conflagrations ended up in Israeli victories. Israel had only to lose one war in order for her to lose her entire country as the Arab countries would not be happy until the last Jew left the Middle East.

In 1967 Nasser told the United Nations to remove its forces from the Sinai Peninsula and the Gaza Strip, and then blockaded the Red Sea thus preventing Israel from continuing with her overseas trade. Israel pre-emptively struck out, and defeated the Arab nations by taking over the Sinai Peninsula, Jerusalem, the Golan Heights and the West Bank. Israel received arms support from the US while Syria and Egypt were supplied by the Soviet Union. Each Arab -Israeli War seemed to make Israel stronger and increased the size of her territory.

The other prominent feature of post-World War II Middle East was the need for oil by all the nations of the world. Saudi Arabia, Iran and other smaller nations of the Middle East were the world's largest producers and they were getting rich from their oil supplies. After the 1973 Israel-Arab War Saudi Arabia and the other Middle Eastern oil-producing lands set up an embargo. They stopped supplying oil to the United States because of her support and arms assistance to Israel. The US suffered a severe shortage of gasoline with long lines of cars waiting to fill up at gas stations. The price of oil rose precipitously and lasted a long time thereafter. This was followed by a recession in the country.

In the early 2010s, as a result of poor living conditions and general dissatisfaction in Arab lands the Arab Spring movement developed. It started in Tunisia and spread like wild –fire throughout the Middle East. The masses of demonstrators were unable to communicate very well through the press, but they discovered a new weapon – the internet and Facebook – where they could instantaneously spread information to friends and all the people. The Arab Spring started off as peaceful demonstrations demanding democracy, and they succeeded in overthrowing a few leaders, such as Hosni Mubarak in Egypt and the leaders of Tunisia, Libya (Muammar Qaddafi) and Bahrain. However, this peaceful revolution of the people calling for democracy and better living conditions developed into a revolution where strong men grabbed the reins of power, as in Egypt, which was taken over by Sisi, an army officer, and in Syria, where Assad attacked and killed many of his own people. The original purpose of the revolution altered entirely, leaving the democracy seekers behind. Russia helped Assad bomb his Syrian people while the US unwittingly assisted him by bombing ISIS strongholds within Syria which made Assad and Iran very happy to see others doing their work for them. Hezbollah was also fighting in the Syrian revolution helping to kill Assad's enemies. What a strange collection of allies in the Syrian revolution – Syria, Iran, Russia, Hezbollah and the US (unwittingly helping Assad by bombing ISIS strongholds)! This revolution as well as the upheavals in other Middle Eastern lands has caused a population shift of millions. There are hundreds of thousands of Middle Easterners living as refugees in Turkey, Jordan, Lebanon and Iraq. They live in tents and other temporary structures, they have no jobs, are not accepted as citizens in their new homes and have no vote and are voiceless. A major humanitarian crisis!

Hezbollah is another story. It is a country within a country. The families of Hezbollah live in Lebanon which originally was a Christian Maronite country. It has a Maronite president, a Sunni prime minister and a Shia speaker of the House, in order to be fair to all sections of the population. Hezbollah has its own army even though its host country (Lebanon) has a national army. Hezbollah says it is fighting to protect Syria and Lebanon from the Sunnis. Hezbollah is a Shiite group supported financially and militarily by Iran and Syria. Even though they hate the Sunnis they assist and train Hamas militants, who live in the Gaza Strip, preparing them to fight against Israel. While Israel withdrew its forces from the Gaza Strip Hamas militants attacked them with bombs and missiles on their way out, and in subsequent days they bombed Israeli cities near the Gaza borders. It appears as though peace talks with Israel are not even on their agenda. A few years ago Israel invaded and bombed Lebanon to try and put an end to Hezbollah attacks on their territory, but this military excursion ended in a stalemate. Hezbollah has been supplied with rockets by Iran that are able to reach just about any city in Israel.

At this time there appears to be a re-alignment taking place in the Middle East. Ever since Israel was declared a State most of her Arab neighbors have gone to war with her on a few occasions or have demanded withdrawal from Arab land. All Arab states were sympathetic towards the lot and the suffering of the Palestinians. Despite the fact that on three different occasions Israel has been willing to return most of the West Bank and all of Gaza to the Palestinians they have refused to accept the offer. On each occasion the Palestinians have been dissatisfied with the arrangements, and now they no longer appear to be interested in even coming to the negotiation table. Ever since the creation of the State of Israel in 1948 they were supported by their neighboring Arab states who also boycotted Israel. They sympathized with the Palestinians and would not allow Israelis to visit their territories, nor would they trade with Israel or even allow Israeli planes to fly over their lands.

The world is changing. At present, the fight between Sunni and Shia that has been continuing for about thirteen hundred years seems to be more prominent in the minds of the Arabs than the Palestine-Israel problem. The Sunnis of the Arab world fear the Shia of Iran. They are afraid of Iran's belligerence, aerial and bombing attacks and their attempts at developing a nuclear device. Persians and Arabs have been enemies for hundreds of years. Israel, too, is watching Iran very carefully, and has already destroyed some of Iran's nuclear capabilities via cyber-attacks. Iran has declared that Israel must be removed from the face of the earth. Some Middle Eastern Arab states have recognized that Israel could be a great support for them as a defense against Iranian aggression. Israel, too, has nuclear capabilities, a fine Army and Air Force which could act as a deterrent to Iran. Amongst all their neighbors only Israel might be able to stand against Iran and save them.

Anwar Sadat made peace with Israel in 1978 at the Camp David Accords after three major wars against them, but was unfortunately assassinated by his own people for doing so. Not long after that Jordan, too, made peace with Israel. Both received large tracts of land in exchange for peace – Sadat received the Sinai Peninsula and Jordan received some border corrections with additions of land.

Recently the United Arab Emirates and Bahrain have signed trade treaties with Israel, and there will be flights and visiting rights between the people of those countries. Saudi Arabia has allowed Israeli planes to fly over its territory. There is also talk of other Arab countries wishing to negotiate similar treaties. Of course, all this is to the displeasure of the Palestine Authority! Yet it is strange to hear of Arab-Israeli friendship and business dealings following seventy years of confrontational animosity. The Palestinians were so sure that the Arab world would forever stand by them, so they felt that they could take their time in making crucial decisions. It almost paid them not to have a land of their own while receiving financial assistance from the United Nations and the US. They had been getting sympathy from the Arab world and many other countries while waiting for Israel to destroy itself or be destroyed. Therefore, they never felt the urgency to make decisions. In the meantime the world was moving along. Iran became an existential threat, Middle Eastern oil became less valuable (the US produces more than Saudi Arabia), there is a move away from fossil fuels and there is a re-alignment of power in the Middle East. The Palestinians seem to have fallen behind.

A major problem is that any possibility of Israel-Palestinian peace talks appear to be on nobody's mind, and a Two-State solution is almost inconceivable at present. The new friendship with other Arab states has placed a damper on Israel's relationship with the Palestinians. Time waits for no man!

APARTHEID

—◆—

I N 1652 THE DUTCH EAST India Company sent Jan van Riebeeck to the
Cape at the tip of South Africa to set up a halfway house – a refreshment
station – in order to supply ships that were rounding the Cape on their long
voyages to the East. The sailors had been getting ill on the ships, and many
were suffering severely as a result of scurvy due to a lack of Vitamin C.
There were no fresh fruit and vegetables available on these long trips to the
Orient. Gardens had to be set up and sailors were to be supplied with the
freshly grown products. It was not until the 18th century when occupation
of the Cape became more pronounced. Many Dutch settlers arrived, as
well as French Huguenots who had been persecuted by the Catholics, and
later, some Germans. The settlers, generally, were a religious people, mostly
Calvinist. They were farmers, known as Boers, which was the Dutch name
for farmers. As in the settlement of North America, the White Man's
diseases infected the native population which had no immunity against
these illnesses, such as measles and small pox. Hence the introduction of
slaves by the Dutch from the Dutch East Indies, mostly Malaya, to assist
in the work.

All went well for a while, until Napoleon Bonaparte started invading
the European countries. Britain sent her navy to the Cape in 1806 in order
to protect the Dutch colony from a possible attack by Napoleon. She took
over the territory in order to protect it, despite resistance from the Boers.
But they forgot to give it back after Napoleon was defeated. The Boers
were unhappy under the British. They did not like to be ruled and they
did not like their laws. When the British liberated their slaves, they were
most dissatisfied, especially when they saw how small a compensation they
received. There were multiple border wars with the surrounding Black
tribes, in which their cattle were stolen and many lives were lost. To add

insult to injury the British brought in a large number of settlers, known as the 1820 Settlers, loyal to the British Crown, who moved to the eastern part of the Cape Province. They brought with them a new language, which also became the language of the laws and promulgations of the land, which they did not like. Obviously, the Boers and the Settlers did not co-operate with each other. Life was becoming too tough with rulers whom they did not wish to obey, and with raids from the tribesmen. The Boers felt that they had to go.

They trekked. There were a series of Treks, the largest of which was the Great Trek. They were known as Voortrekkers, which means Pioneers. They and their families traveled by ox-wagon. They traveled north and east. When they came across African tribesmen who seemed hostile they placed their ox-wagons in a circle, all men, women and children remaining within the circle for protection, and they fired at the on-coming enemy through the wheels of the ox-wagons. They traveled through valleys, crossed rivers and mountains through fair weather and foul, wagons broke down and had to be repaired, food had to be found and prepared as they passed through unfriendly territory. They entered Natal, where they met the Zulu chief, Dingaan, who invited them to his kraal so he could tell them about the land which he was going to donate to them. When they arrived, Dingaan and his men fell upon them, killing as many as they could.

Finally, they crossed the Orange River and set up a republic called the Orange Free State. Others crossed the Vaal River and set up the South African Republic, also known as the Transvaal. At last, they were free of the British. This freedom did not last long because the Boers were having trouble with the South African native tribes. Again, there were attacks and cattle thefts, and it was difficult to hold the tribesmen back. The authorities had very little money and assets, and were losing whatever they had very fast. The British said that the Boer Republics were unstable, ungovernable, bankrupt and facing civil war. With that reasoning, they marched in and took over the suzerainty of the Republics. They allowed them to run their own domestic affairs, but the British took over in the handling of the tribes around them and in matters relating to foreign affairs.

The First Boer War took place in 1880 as a result of the desire for expansion by the British Empire and the hatred of the Boers for British domination over their lives. Petty arguments and squabbles expanded into Boers attacking British stations. In fact, this was the first war that Britain lost since her loss of the American colonies in the 1776-1783 War of Independence. The Boers won back their independence.

In 1886 gold was discovered in an unforsaken and sparsely inhabited area of the Transvaal. At this site a city was built, Johannesburg, a city where the inhabitants had gold under their feet; a city that became the second largest city in Africa in just a few years. The gold deposits ran on for over a hundred miles along the Witwatersrand in the southern Transvaal and stretching in to the Orange Free State. This was the largest gold deposit ever found on the earth. Speculators arrived from all over South Africa, and then from all over the world in order to make a profit from these gold reserves. They came to live in Johannesburg, and, as a result, Johannesburg, was occupied almost entirely by foreigners who made huge demands from the President Paul Kruger of the Transvaal. They wanted equal rights and they wanted the vote. Paul Kruger was not willing to give this large influx of foreigners (known as Uitlanders) equal status as citizens or the vote – and, probably, be voted out of power by them. Paul Kruger did nothing to satisfy the demands of the Uitlanders.

In 1895 Starr Jameson conducted a raid, which was probably set up by Cecil Rhodes who was Prime Minister of the Cape Province. The Jameson Raid was meant to enter the gold fields, whereby the Uitlanders would join him and help to overthrow the Transvaal government. However, it was an utter disaster. The Jameson raiders arrived, but the Uitlanders did not come to Johannesburg to fight – they came for gold. The Jameson Raiders were rounded up, arrested and sentenced to the embarrassment of the British. The gold mines flourished and South Africa was by far the largest supplier of gold in the world. She was also the largest producer of diamonds in the world, as these expensive gems were discovered in Kimberley a few years before that. You can visualize what a wonderful prize adoption of Transvaal into the British Empire would be. Britain could not take her eyes off this wealthy young country.

After a century of conflicts between the Boers and the Britons it seemed inevitable that a war would break out. It did, and is known as the Second Boer War. The British maintained that they wanted to protect the rights of the Uitlanders and they also wanted to see better treatment of the Black population – no mention of the gold and diamonds which were probably the major causes of the war.

The British set up outposts all around the Transvaal causing Paul Kruger to feel uncomfortable. He asked Britain to remove these outposts. He allowed them 48 hours to do so, but when nothing was done about shutting them, he sent his men out on the attack. They immediately besieged Ladysmith in Natal and Mafeking and Kimberley in the Cape Province. Of course, Britain was five thousand miles away and had been suddenly surprised by the sieges. They soon mobilized and sent men from all corners of the Empire. Britain fielded an army of a half million men whereas the Boers could scarcely muster about 80,000. The British army consisted of uniformed and trained soldiers.

The Boers did not possess a trained military presence. Most of their men had never seen service, but knew how to use a gun and how to take care of themselves. They knew the terrain – it was their terrain. All the people living on the land were their people who would do anything to help them. They would hide their men and they would stow away the equipment that their men had stolen from the British in their night raids. This was the beginning of guerilla warfare. These men did not march or respond to bugles. They came out at night, raided British outposts and became invisible by day, hiding in the homesteads, being sheltered on the farms while appearing to be farm-hands and being fed and taken care of by the host for that particular day. They were here today, and gone tomorrow. These slippery and scarcely seen guerillas could seldom be tied down. This war continued from 1899 to 1902 – a small band of guerillas fighting the British Empire in the most expensive war that Britain had ever fought. The British began a scorched earth policy, starving out the Boers wherever they could. In fact, there were times when the Black tribesmen were competing with the Boers for foraging whatever was still available for harvesting. The British placed tens of thousands of women, children and men who were not able to join the Boer forces in concentration camps where numerous people died from malnutrition, bad sanitation, lack of clean water and conditions such as typhoid and other infectious diseases.

One lesson that the British learnt was about the use of horses for war duties. Three hundred thousand horses died during the Second Boer War while in attendance to the British forces. Some died at sea on their passage to South Africa. Some died of excessive weight put on their backs to carry equipment. Many died of war injuries. Consequently, the British decided that horses should no longer be used in combat. Fortunately, soon after automobile engines, trucks and tanks were developed. Another lesson that they learnt was taught to them by the Boers. Guerilla warfare, as fought by the Boers was a "pain in the neck" to the British. It has been practiced by many armies in the world since then, but the British also caught on to it, and have used it since.

Then suddenly the war was over. The Boers in the battle areas looked at each other and asked why? They were not losing. They were certainly creating havoc behind the British lines. Why should the war be stopped when things were going well? The Boers wanted to continue the fight in order to avenge the deaths of their comrades, the cruelty of the concentration camps and their general deep-seated hatred for the British. Apparently, some of the Boer leaders, including General Smuts, got together and decided that there had been a great deal of loss of life on both sides. Yes, they were doing well against the British, but this small band of guerillas was not going to beat the British Empire fielding 500,000 troops with millions more in reserve. They should sue for peace, they suggested; so, they crossed the enemy lines and surrendered! The Treaty of Vereeniging was later signed.

The Treaty put an end to the two Boer Republics, Transvaal and the Orange Free State. They were absorbed into the British Empire with the promise of self-government. Many farmers tried to return to the land after the war, but found it impossible to do so because of the British scorched earth policy, and many others did not even attempt to go back to their farms. The same applies to the tribes, as they, too, suffered as a result of the scorched earth policy. The agrarian nature of the country was changing, as these people needed work. Where could they go? The mines required laborers, and so the Boers and the Blacks left the farms and went to the mines where gold was being produced in ever increasing amounts every year. There were also mining-allied industries which were developing.

The Union of South Africa became a member of the British Empire in 1910. Two of the Boer generals - Louis Botha and Jan Smuts - became staunch friends of Britain. Both of them became Prime Ministers of South Africa, and both played large roles in aiding the British in the two world wars. However, there was a problem at the beginning of World War I when the Maritz Rebellion broke out. There was a majority of Afrikaners (who had always been called Boers in the past) who could not shake off their anti-British attitudes. They were the "bitter-enders". Why should we fight on the side of the British who have forever been our enemy? they asked. We should rather fight for the Germans; they helped us in the Boer War. This rebellion was soon put to an end, but they and their off-spring became the roots of the Nationalist Party who resisted service in the Second World War – many were sent to jail for anti-government activities. They were the implementers of the policy of apartheid after the Second World War and they turned South Africa into a Republic. They were also responsible for South Africa's exit from the British Empire. Finally, it was the Nationalist Party who lost the election in 1994 and passed the government on to the African National Congress, led by Nelson Mandela.

During the Second World War General Smuts was Prime Minister of the country. He had become an Anglophile since the end of the Boer War. Immediately after Britain declared war on Germany he did the same, but he had to be careful, however, as the majority of the Afrikaners were anti-British, and there would be a problem getting them to fight on the side of Britain. Wisely, he said that South Africa would not send troops to fight in Europe, but it would go to war in order to drive Fascism out of Africa. South African troops spread up the east coast of Africa, freeing Somalia and Abyssinia from the Italian forces (Mussolini was Hitler's ally). Thereupon they went to North Africa, and fought under Montgomery against Rommel and his German and Italian armies. Once Africa was cleared of Fascism, most of the South African forces returned home, although some went on to fight in Italy.

All this time General Smuts had been on the British War Cabinet, such was the British respect for their old enemy of the Boer War. Back in South Africa acts of terrorism were being inflicted on government installations by followers of the Nationalist Party. Many of their leaders spent much of the war in jail. At the general election at the end of the war General Smuts was defeated by Dr. Malan, the leader of the Nationalist Party. Smuts received the same gratitude (or lack thereof) that Winston Churchill received in Britain after having been responsible, more than any other single person, for having defeated the Nazis. South Africa was now ruled by the Nationalist Party.

There had always been racism in South Africa, similar to the racism in the United States. It was present under the Boers, under the British administration and under the Botha and Smuts governments. It had always been tacit, and often not legislated or referred to very much but always present. Now the Nationalist government made it a cause celebre. A future Prime Minster, Dr, Hendrik Verwoerd – who was not born in South Africa, but born in the Netherlands – introduced the policy of Apartheid (separate-ness). All Blacks were classified as belonging to a Homeland, which was an area within South Africa from whence their tribe originated. The Homelands, the government told the Non-White population, would be developed and industrialized. Their homelands would become developed and industrialized like the White areas, only separate but equal. These areas never developed; they remained separate and unequal. Dr. Verwoerd described apartheid as a "policy of good neighbors", which it was not.

For those non-Whites who worked in the city, they had to live in designated areas outside the city. The city was for Whites while the townships were for Blacks. 90% of the land was for Whites who were 20% of the population, and 10% of the land was for Blacks who were 80% of the population. There was dominance of the Afrikaner minority in every aspect of life. Pass laws and influx control were very important. No Black person could be seen on the streets unless he was carrying a 'pass' from his White employer giving him permission to be off the property until a specified time. Most of the people in jails were for non-observance of the pass laws. Segregation and restriction of movement were legal. Whereas in the past many Blacks had been living in the cities they were now forced, by the hundreds of thousands, to move out of the cities and into the townships and Homelands. Long and expensive commutes to the work-place in the cities followed. There were no cultural facilities or public spaces in the townships. Public transportation for Whites and Blacks were separate; water fountains, queues at the bank and other facilities, too, were separate. Movie theaters, restaurants and all places of entertainment were for Whites only. Mixed marriages were banned and miscegenation was against the law.

Into this setting arrived Nelson Mandela. He was a Xhosa, belonging to the Thembu tribe, born in Mvezo in the Eastern Cape Province. His great grandfather was once the King of the Thembu. His father was the councillor to the monarch. When his father died, he was placed under the guardianship of the monarch. He received a good education in nearby Qunu, and was then sent to Fort Hare University, a college for Blacks. He did not graduate as he was thrown out of school for joining a student protest group. When he came home again the King was furious and said that either he return to school or marry a woman that the King had chosen for him. He rejected both choices, and with the King's son ran away to Johannesburg. They spent some time working as security guards on a gold mine. Then Nelson went to university to study law, but he did not complete his studies – he said that he was not a good student even though he loved education. He met Walter Sisulu, who was a big voice in the African National Congress, who found him a job with a group of practicing lawyers. He also married at this time.

He became active in the ANC, displaying bitter opposition to the racism in the country. He read books by Marx, Lenin and Mao, and became interested in following the non-violent resistance of Mahatma Gandhi. At this stage he was elected the ANC leader in the Transvaal. In 1952 he was arrested and jailed under the Suppression of Communism Act. After bearing a few children his wife left him because of his pre-occupation with politics and seldom coming home. Soon after that he met Winnie, who was a political activist, and fitted in well with his political ideas and plans. They married and produced children.

In 1956 he, amongst many others in the ANC, was arrested and accused of high treason because they were accused of advocating violent revolution. The accused asked and were granted a change in the three judges chosen for the case as they were considered to be members of the Nationalist Party. When the verdict was finally delivered by the three new judges, they were declared to be not guilty as they could not be proved to be Communist nor had there been evidence of violent attempts at overthrowing the government.

As an act against the hated Pass Laws many Blacks were seen burning their passes in public. In 1960 at Sharpeville large crowds were demonstrating outside the police station against the Pass Laws. The police fired at them, killing 69 people. It was realized by the leadership of the

ANC after the tragedy of Sharpeville that non-violent demonstrations would be of no avail against the government of apartheid. Mandela, it was agreed upon, would form a militant wing of the ANC called the Spear of the Nation (uMkhonte we Sizwe). They only attacked government targets and avoided the loss of life wherever they could. They caused a fair amount of damage, and were declared to be a terrorist organization by South Africa and the United States.

The Rivonia Trial of 1963 was the beginning of a chain of events that changed South Africa forever. Twelve highly placed ANC members and members of the Spear of the Nation were arrested in a raid by the police at Lilliesleaf Farm in Rivonia, a suburb of Johannesburg, and charged under the Sabotage Act of sabotage and attempting to overthrow the government, which could invoke the death penalty. The ANC had been banned three years prior to the raid. The Trial brought world attention to the apartheid laws of the country, which had hitherto been overlooked by the major countries of the globe. All the saboteurs were given life imprisonment. Nelson Mandela spent 27 years in jail.

He spent the first 18 years in jail on the cold wind-swept Robben Island off Cape Town. All political prisoners were involved in rock breaking. At nights he was busy studying by correspondence course for a law degree through the University of London. He encouraged his co-prisoners to do the same – not to waste their time and to study for something.

Prisoners were forced to wear short pants. Mandela demanded that they be allowed to wear long pants if they wanted to because he said that short pants made them look school-boyish and vulnerable, and he did not want to be left in such a position. His demand was granted. One of the ANC prisoners had a knack of being able to write very small and legibly. The prisoners would meet in secret, and a tiny note would be thrown over the yard wall. Somebody chosen from outside would come along later in the day, pick up the message and send it to ANC headquarters. In this manner they were able to maintain contact with the African National Congress.

In 1980 people began saying out aloud and placing posters all over South Africa, "Free Mandela". The United Nations Security Council called for his release. Yet President Reagan and Margaret Thatcher of Britain considered him a terrorist and a Communist sympathizer. It must be remembered that the Cold War was taking place. Britain and the US were anti-Communist, and South Africa was considered as a bulwark against Communism in Africa. Britain and the US were trading with South Africa and were involved in gold mining, industrial and business enterprises in the country.

In 1982, after 18 years on Robben Island, Mandela was transferred to the Pollsmoor prison in Cape Town, and later he was sent to the Victor Verster prison in Paarl, where he was given a suite of his own. He was allowed to grow his own garden; he was given a chef, and, generally, living was made easier for him. A tailor was sent to him to measure and fit him for suits, and he was allowed to be visited by some members of the government and foreign dignitaries. He was even taken for the occasional drive to visit some of the local scenery. When the driver stopped the car and went to get them some food, he never ran away even though he could have tried to do so. The world was beginning to show an interest in the "Free Mandela" movement. Sanctions and boycotts were put in place against South Africa, investment from the outside stopped, even international sports teams would not play against South Africa. Being a country that loved sport, this hurt very much.

In 1985 President P.K. Botha offered to release Mandela if he promised to abandon all forms of violence. Mandela answered that he would only accept freedom without any restrictions. He was also told that he could have his freedom and the ANC would be legalized. Again he said, he would accept those terms only if the government renounced violence. So, he remained in prison. In the meantime he heard that his wife, Winnie Mandela, had established ownership of a soccer team which, other than playing soccer, were used by her for assassinating people who were her enemies. He did not like what he had heard, but he did nothing about it. After all, while he and the leaders were in jail, Winnie had kept up with anti-government statements and actions- she had kept the 'ball rolling'.

At Wembley Stadium in London a world-wide concert was held in honor of "Free Mandela". Two hundred million people saw and heard this concert on their television sets. F.W. de Klerk became the new Prime Minister, and he freed Mandela unconditionally and legalized the African National Congress. He had heard the outcry from the world, and South Africa was suffering from sanctions and boycotts. Thereafter Mandela went on a world tour, visiting many countries, and meeting many heads of State. Strangely, the one land he did not visit was the USSR. He had been accused of being a Communist and had been a member of the Communist Party at one stage. He met Qaddaffi of Libya, Arafat of the PLO and Castro of Cuba. People asked of him "How could you embrace such people who were terrorists and anti-democratic?" He replied "They were there to help me when I needed a friend. Where were you when the apartheid government was persecuting us? Many of you were on their side!"

In April 1994 Nelson Mandela became the first Black President democratically elected by the people of South Africa. It was the first time in the history of the country that Black people had been allowed to vote in an election. Imagine such a situation – an impossible dream! A Black people who had for centuries been considered as a sub-human species, who were poor and discriminated against, not permitted to reside where White people lived or to occupy positions at the work-place which had been reserved for their White counterparts, who owned no property and who were at the lowest end of the social scale, were now the new leaders of the country. The White bosses who were the minority of the population, the wealthy and the educated, subjects of the most powerful nation in Africa, one of the few nations with enough knowledge and know-how to produce and own nuclear weaponry – these people were now devoid of political power. The Black people on a Black continent had triumphed against their White bosses, those people who considered them to be incapable of anything but manual labor. Both Mandela and de Klerk received the Nobel Peace Prize for bringing a peaceful termination to the apartheid struggle.

The Boers had arrived in an unexplored section of the African content. They had opened up the hinterland, and fought against the British and invading tribes along their borders. They had no friends. In a few hundred years they built up a nation, developed a language, a literature, scientific advances, arts and culture, a large protective army and air force. They simply walked away from the control wheels of government like good sportsmen, and departed into the background without a whimper. They asked the International Atomic Commission to dismantle their nuclear weapons. Nobody expected the Nationalist Party to give up so easily and to walk away so quietly from what their ancestors and they had fought for and protected all their lives. Everything that was sacred to them was surrendered. Opposition from them is almost non-existent. What a surprise! This, from a people who ruled with an iron hand!

The new South African government under Mandela tried something that had never been tried before. With the help of Bishop Desmond Tutu, they set up a Truth and Reconciliation Committee rather than indict and try some of the perpetrators of the cruelties of the apartheid regime. Mandela and Tutu felt that in order to bring the country, Black and White, together it would not be helpful to impose large sentences – imprisonment and execution – upon those found guilty. Understanding and forgiveness might be better than revenge for the future of the country. Victims of gross human rights violations were invited to tell their stories and perpetrators of injustice were asked to explain themselves. Some withheld the truth and some must have lied, but the Commission probably succeeded to a large extent. There were some flaws, and many victims were angry about perpetrators receiving amnesty. Many Blacks felt that it was far too easy for those who had committed heinous crimes – all they had to do was to tell their story (often hiding some of the truths), apologize and look sorry, and, literally, get away with murder! Many of the perpetrators named other people who were involved, rather than appear to be alone in the crime. They wanted to show that they were only small wheels in a larger operation.

The Truth and Reconciliation Commission was a contrast to the Nuremberg Trials which saw a handing out of prison sentences and executions. Is justice a prerequisite for reconciliation? It may take a long time before the experts can decide such a difficult question.

There are many Africans who forgot that Mandela brought them into the 'promised land'. They believe that he conceded too much by allowing a continued control of the economy by the Whites. Despite having spent a life-time fighting the inequality between the White and Black populations Mandela had a respect for his nemesis. He respected their education and the advances they had made. He wanted equality and a partnership with them. However, the reason for the peaceful transition from the apartheid regime to a democratic government was because of the compromises. That is why there was no race war or economic collapse. In countries like Zimbabwe where there were no such compromises made with the White government, farmers were removed from their lands, agricultural and tobacco production went downhill, Whites were attacked and pushed while the economy was in dire trouble, and, all the time, getting worse.

What were the gains resulting from the overthrow of apartheid? The Republic of South Africa became a democratic country for the first time in its history. Racism came to an end and equal rights for all people were instituted. People from all countries cheered the victory of Mandela. He became one of the most loved heroes of the entire world.

However, many promises were left unfulfilled. If one looks around the country it might seem as though apartheid still exists. Poverty is rife; the middle class has slightly increased in numbers, but not by much; unemployment is high while crime has greatly increased. People have surrounded their homes with high walls and are guarded by large dangerous dogs. There appears to be insufficient police to handle the problems. Anarchy is on the rise. The government has shifted money away from housing and development for the common man to the erection of high-profile malls and museums in poor areas. There are obvious gaps in the development of White areas and Black areas, even though there are far more Blacks now living in White areas. The numbers of squatters sleeping over in public areas are expanding. Crime and the incidence of AIDS are considered to be amongst the highest in the world. The economy is on a downward trend. At the end of the Apartheid Era there was great elation amongst the people because freedom and democracy had finally arrived, but that elation seems to have somewhat dwindled amidst despair. South Africa has become more like a Third World Country despite the fact that the evil system of Apartheid has been crushed.

There are very few 'poor Whites' in the country whereas poverty amongst the Black population has increased. Despite the fall of apartheid, the poor seem to be stuck in a rut. The World Bank has said that South Africa is the most unequal nation on the planet. There is bribery and corruption within the African National Congress; a recent President was indicted on charges of bribery and corruption. Because of the lack of improvement in the lives of most individuals there is voter apathy. Desmond Tutu, the Anglican bishop and a great friend of Mandela as well as a fighter against apartheid while it existed, has said that he would not vote for the ANC at the next election. He actually stated that he was glad that Mandela was dead because this way he was not aware of the extent of how low the ANC, his Party, had fallen. He regarded Mandela as a moral beacon, and that the ANC leaders had learnt nothing from his example.

Apartheid was government sponsored racism practiced as a national policy against a group of people of a different color. Just as Empires have been and are on the way out, so has apartheid been expelled from South Africa. Racism still occurs amongst many countries all over the world, but hopefully they will in time go the way of apartheid.

Apparently, the removal of the 'parasite' of apartheid that had been sucking and gnawing into the bones of the Black population of South Africa did not instantaneously herald a miraculous cure. There is hope that the lot of the people will improve in time. With wisdom and better governance their lives should change for the better.

THE SCAPEGOAT

THE JEWS HAVE SURVIVED AS a nation and as a religion for over thirty-five hundred years. It has been a bitter uphill journey most of the way. They were supposed to have been God's Chosen People, but if you look at their history it appears more like the Journey of the Damned. They have encountered insurmountable numbers of obstacles during their existence, yet they are still here to tell their story despite the fact that most, if not all, the nations of the Bible have succumbed. Despite all the signs of gradual disappearance off the face of the earth there appears to be a strong re-growth in Israel. The language of Hebrew which has been dormant for thousands of years (except in religious texts) has come back to life and the Land of Israel has been re-born.

Yet, beyond Israel, throughout the Diaspora, Judaism, as a religion appears to be suffering because having left the shtetel and the ghetto Jews are having increased contact with non-Jews and are marrying outside the religion, thus depleting the numbers. Consider the loss of six million Jews as a result of the Holocaust and add that to the numerical loss from the marriages outside the religion, we can see that there is a problem.

Through the preceding millennia Jews have been the targets of attack from many people. Have you ever kicked your dog under the table when you were very upset? If so, you found a scapegoat. The dog had nothing to do with your state of misery but you needed an outlet for your frustrations, and the poor dog just happened to be in the way. Anti-Semitism is a form of hostility toward or discrimination against Jews. It, too, is an outlet. The word (anti-Semitism) is a misnomer as Arabs, too, are Semites, yet anti-Semitism does not refer to them. In fact, Arabs could be anti-Semites by hating Jews without hating themselves. Nazis were well-known anti-Semites. They not only cast their hate upon Jews, but also upon Christians whose ancestors had been Jewish since three generations before. Leon Pinsker, an early Zionist in the 20th century used the term Judeophobe rather than anti-Semite.

Some have considered Judas as a typical representative of the Jews who was supposed to have 'sold out' Jesus for a handful of silver, displaying love for money rather than loyalty to his teacher and leader. The Crucifixion was responsible for Christiaan anti-Semitism for the last two thousand years. The New Testament accuses the Jews for the execution of Jesus while it downplays the role of the Romans and Pontius Pilate. God, it said, was murdered by the right hand of Israel. Even though the order of crucifixion was given by Pontius Pilate, who said thereafter "I am innocent of this man's blood. It is your responsibility", Jews have taken the brunt of the guilt. The Christian Church taught for two thousand years that the Jews committed deicide. Not until late in the 20th century did the 2nd Vatican Council repudiate the collective guilt of the Jews for the death of Jesus.

Jews in Europe were considered by their fellow countrymen to be different. The European people said that Jews were disconnected from the rest of the population, they were self-made outcasts, dressed strangely, were aloof and arrogant and did not adapt to the values of non-Jews. They were forced to wear a badge or some other sign to notify non-Jews that they belonged to some form of sub-species. Non-Jews were also jealous of them for their artistic and musical ability, their intelligence and their supposed wealth. They were considered to be disloyal to their country because they prayed "Next year in Jerusalem".

Soon after the Israelites under the leadership of Moses crossed the Red Sea in their flight from slavery in Egypt, they came across their first anti-Semitic attack in the Sinai Desert. The Amalakites fell upon them and tried to destroy them. The Amalekites were the descendants of Esau, the less preferred twin brother of Jacob. Esau sold his birthright to Jacob for a handful of red potage, and went to sojourn in the desert while harboring a hatred for his family. Fortunately, the Children of Israel defended themselves against the Amalekites and survived. Amongst the Jews Amalek is considered to be the epitome of evil. The Torah says the Amalekites must be obliterated and their evil must never be forgotten.

During Biblical days the Jews lived in a land of their own (actually two lands, Israel and Judea). They never had an Empire but Judaism was the root of Christianity and Islam, both of which spread across the world, proselytizing the indigenous populations. Today each of these religions has well over a billion subjects and they are the two largest religions in the world. Yet despite the influence that the Jewish population had in the formation of these two religions and despite the influence it has today on the sciences, medicine, arts and philosophy the Jewish population is, comparatively speaking, tiny.

When the Greeks took control of the Holy Land they expected the Jews to worship their gods but they refused to do so because they believed in only one God who created heaven and earth, and did not believe in multiple foreign gods. This created a feeling amongst the Greeks that Jews were different and thus alien, unappreciative and disloyal. Despite that, Jews respected the Greeks.

Non-Jews saw the Roman destruction of the Temple many decades later as God's punishment to the Jews for the death of Jesus. Once the Jews had produced Jesus there was no further need for their existence. Their land was in the hands of the Romans, and thus without a land of their own they were now condemned to becoming 'wandering Jews', a people searching for a home. Such an alien, weak and migratory nation, doomed to live on the earth homeless and God-less was fodder for those seeking someone to kick around, a scapegoat. Because they looked pale and sickly for lack of sun, and because they spoke in another tongue and they prayed and practiced rituals in a foreign manner they were targets for the racists. When they arrived in Europe they were in Europe, but not of Europe. These strange people on the outskirts of society, who had killed their God, could be guilty of almost any evil, including the arrival of disasters upon the very people in whose country they were residing, who were giving them shelter and allowing them to live in their land in order to survive. Yes, during the plague epidemic, they were accused of having poisoned the wells, even though they too were drinking from the same wells and dying from the same plague. When a Christian child was missing, the Jews were often blamed for having waylaid and killed him for the purpose of requiring his blood to produce their Passover matzos.

From the 11th to 14th centuries they were forced to live in ghettos in Italy. The ghetto system spread to other European lands. These outcasts were despised and plundered. Anti-Jewish laws were enacted, and pogroms followed in Eastern Europe. In Western Europe the Jews were frequently expelled. Edward I expelled them from England, where they had been rather well integrated, in 1290 for their strange business dealings. However, Oliver Cromwell invited them back in 1656 (three hundred and fifty years later) for the same reason for which they had been expelled – their strange business dealings! This time they were called upon to improve the economy. In fact, they did well on their return to England, and even moved with the English to different parts of the newly developing British Empire – especially the Caribbean islands.

King Philip IV of France drove the Jews out in 1306 when he needed money to fight the Flemish; he made them leave their money and possessions behind after which he sold their possessions and used the money in order to finance his war. They were exiled from France on a few other occasions. King Ferdinand and Queen Isabella of Spain exiled the Jews that did not convert to Catholicism during the Spanish Inquisition starting in 1492.

An entire race is often made to share the guilt of a crime caused by one man. Sometimes the crime of one individual will be blamed on the Jewish state of Israel which may be thousands of miles away from the scene of the crime. Some racists will say "I don't dislike Jews. I only hate Israel". Usually the two are inseparable. The Jews, they will say, are more loyal to Israel than to their host country. Israel, too, is treated by a double standard. Holocaust deniers, despite data, photographs and facts investigated and proven, witnessed, recognized and accepted even by Germany, will either say that there was no Holocaust or the Jews are exaggerating the facts, or are bringing up the subject too frequently and looking for sympathy. The number six million, they contend, is an imagined number. The cost of burial of six million people would add up to huge sums of money, said the father of Mel Gibson, a famous anti-Semite. Do you think the Nazis would spend that amount of money on the people that they despised, he asks! These anti-Semites deny proven facts and set up their own false information as truth.

Anti-Semitism may come from the Right and from the Left. Jews are accused of being both Communists and Capitalists, depending on whether the speaker despises Communists or Capitalists. Others will call Jews ostentatious or avaricious, again depending upon their pet peeve; or they may say that Jews interfere too much in a nation's politics or, the other extreme, that they have no interest in their country. They corrupt culture, say the uncouth; they Judaize it, even though wherever the Jews live culture seems to thrive. There seemed to be one advantage that kings and the noble classes found in the Jews. Neither Christianity nor Islam permit their subjects to practice usury whereas Judaism does not disallow it. Jews have aided kings and emperors with loans to pay their debts and fight their wars, but when it came to re-paying their debts with interest which had been agreed upon, problems often seemed to arise and anti-Semitism began to flare up. Or was this a good time to consider exiling the Jews!?

"The Protocols of the Learned Elders of Zion" was written and published in Russia in the 19th century. It talks of the Jews plotting to dominate and take over the world by war or revolution, and wherever there will be a weakened state the Jews would be there to dominate it. It was the greatest forgery of the century. The czarists before the Communist Revolution believed in the book. Henry Ford believed it and helped to spread the sales of the book in the United States; but then, too late, he changed his mind. Adolph Hitler used it in his defamation of the Jews. It has been proved over and over again to be a hoax and full of lies, and yet in 1987 the Iranian embassy in Brazil, despite knowledge of its lies, was circulating the book. In the 21st century the Arabs in the Middle East are still selling and reading it. In the US Muslims at Wayne State University in Michigan and the University of California at Berkeley were continuing to distribute it, knowing that it was a farce and totally untrue.

During the time of the Crusades the European countries made a combined concentrated effort to re-gain the Holy Places in Jerusalem and the Holy Land. They went to fight the Muslims on a number of occasions, yet on their way to Jerusalem, while still in Europe, they first had to murder as many Jews as they could find, before embarking on the final leg of their Crusade. This, despite the fact that the war was against the Muslims, and not the Jews! When the Crusaders departed for the First Crusade they attacked the Jews of the Rhineland and the Danube, killing them in their homes and in their synagogues. German and French Jews suffered the most. During the fighting that took place for the capture of Jerusalem Jews fought with Saladin and the Muslims to defend the Holy Places.

Many Jews migrated from Western Europe in order to escape persecution, and went to Poland where it had been rumored that Jews were better treated. It turned out to be so. Poland became a home where they studied and prayed, developed schools and lived comfortably. It appeared to be the new Babylon, as after the time when they were exiled from Judea by Nebuchadnezzar. However, after some time persecution and pogroms developed in Poland, especially after it was invaded by Russia, Prussia and Austro-Hungary. Thereafter Poland was divided into three states, and matters went downhill.

Catherine the Great did not allow Jews to live in Russia. There were no Jews living in St. Petersburg, Moscow or any of the other large cities. She allowed them to live along the borders of the Russian Empire in Belorus and Ukraine. They called it the Pale of Settlement. Only after the Communists took over in Russia were the Jews permitted to dwell within the country.

Today, since the advent of the European Union we see an influx of Muslims into Europe. There are a half million Jews in France, but there are five million Muslims living there. Consequently, anti-Semitism in France has increased a great deal. The Yellow Vests are a movement in France who meet every week to complain about fuel prices and other such matters. They turned their hatred towards the Jews, thus helping to spread anti-Semitism. This has happened in other lands, including the Middle East where anti-government rioting develops into anti-Jewish demonstrations. In Hungary, Victor Orban has been venting Jew hatred while Poland, which was Adolph Hitler's willing helper in some of the death camps, has been denying its role during World War II despite numerous recorded incidents. Germany, in its post-World War II period, has been doing its best to make Germany a haven for Jews, but with the influx of Muslims anti-Semitism is on the rise. Likewise, we see much of the same in other European countries. Many Jews have left France and gone to live elsewhere because of the uncertainty of day-to-day living. Ever since the Jews were re-invited to return to England by Oliver Cromwell they have lived there rather peacefully. In fact, the British respected their drive and will to succeed. Of late, the Jews who belonged mostly to the Labor Party, have now left the Labor Party in droves because of anti-Semitism within it, which is being spread by none other than its leader.

SIDNEY OWITZ

Within the United States we have seen an upsurge of White Supremacists and Neo-Nazis marching and ranting against Jews and Blacks. There are organizations in universities and colleges pressuring the authorities for boycotts, divestment and sanctions against Israel, accompanied by demands for cessation of educational and student exchanges. Evangelicals, however, in the US have shown great friendship to Israel, but there seems to be an ulterior motive. Apparently when the Messiah arrives it will only be when Israel is in the hands of the Jews, and thereafter all Jews will turn to Christ!

The inferiority of the Jews was proclaimed by Adolph Hitler before he became Chancellor of Germany. He wrote about the danger of the Jews to Germany in his book "Mein Kampf", and he repeated it ad infinitum after he became Chancellor, while stressing the superiority of the Aryan race. Christians resented Jewish successes and intellectual superiority in Medicine and the Sciences, such as in people like Freud and Einstein. Hitler blamed the Jews for the attempt by the Communists to take over Germany from the Weimar Republic after World War I, and he also blamed them for anything that was not right in Germany. In 1933 he struck out against international Jewry. He discussed his intentions of carrying out his final solution for them. Nazi anti-Semitism progressed in Germany in pre-World War II days culminating in Kristellnacht with the burning and destruction of Jewish homes and stores, and Jews being driven from their homes and the streets. They were ousted from their professions and teaching posts at the universities, the acting stage and the orchestras. He made their lives miserable. He killed them in the streets, he killed them in concentration camps, he killed them wherever he found them. At the Wannsee Conference in 1942 we heard his Final Solution for the Jews. His intention was to eliminate the Jewish population from the earth. Thus followed the greatest destruction of a people by a civilized nation in the history of the world – the Holocaust! He was responsible for the deaths of six million Jews.

Alan Dershowitz said that Hitler did not do this alone. He received aid from his willing helpers in most countries of Europe who co-operated with him in World War II. When he called for the Jews from the occupied countries to be delivered to his death camps for mass extermination the leaders responded with alacrity.

For almost two thousand years the Catholic Church has been the forerunner of anti-Semitism. In Italy, while Pope Pius IX (a known anti-Semite) was the leader of the Church in the 19th century, Jews were expected to convert to Catholicism, or else they were told that they would be very sorry if they did not. By that they meant that they would reside in a 'living Hell' and when they died they would go to Hell.

There have been many cases in nineteenth century Italy when a Jewish boy, on his way to Hebrew school or a friend's house, was waylaid by a priest or non-priest, taken in to the Church and baptized without his consent. This baptism was considered to be permanent by the Church, and was done, supposedly, for the sake of the unfortunate child.

One night in the city of Bologna, the Mortara family who were Jewish, were sitting down to dinner when a member of the Carbonari walked in and asked which one of the children was Edgardo. Edgardo was the six-year old, the youngest of the children, born in 1851. He was identified by the family members, whereupon the Carbonari person said "I have to take him with me". Aghast, they all asked why, and the answer was "I don't know. I am only obeying orders". Edgardo cried, the children tried to protect their brother, the parents pleaded for an explanation, but it was of no avail. Amid tears and screaming, Edgardo was dragged out of the house. Where was he being taken? The officer said he did not know, but the authorities would contact them. Days turned into weeks, which soon became months, and the parents were not given any information as to where Edgardo had been taken.

Apparently, some time before the kidnapping of Edgardo he had been ill and the parents employed a young woman as a maid to assist them in taking care of him and the house. She grew to love Edgardo very much, and then she thought that if this beautiful and clever child should die from his illness he would go to Hell, as she well knew that was the place where non-believers in Jesus would finally go. And that would be such a terrible thing to happen to this wonderful child. One day when Edgardo recovered from his illness the mother asked the maid to take him for a walk to the grocery store down the road in order to buy some things that she required. At the same time Edgardo would be able to get some fresh air. The maid took Edgardo with her, and while she was talking to the grocer she recounted to him the child's illness adding "What a pity it would have been if this child had died? He would have gone to Hell because he is a Jew." The grocer, a religious Catholic agreed, and said "It could still happen to him on some future date. Why don't you baptize him?" The maid replied that it would be impossible to bring a priest to his Jewish home. The grocer told her that a priest was not required for baptism. Anybody could do it if he or she were a Catholic and knew the prayer. In fact he brought out the correct book and the necessary water for baptism, told her how to do it and what to say, and within a few minutes Edgardo was baptized and had become a Christian. And the grocer said "This is forever! And there is no way to undo the act!" This baptism was reported to the Catholic Church.

A few years elapsed after the Carbonari took Edgardo away before the parents were called and were told that they could visit him in Rome, at the Catechumen, a place where converts to Catholicism were taken to live and were trained into becoming religious Catholics. The parents and siblings arrived to meet Edgardo. There were tears and kissing and hugging, and when they said to Edgardo "Come home with us!" he said "Not unless you become Catholics. I cannot live in a Jewish home." That was a shock. The parents had no desire of ever converting away from Judaism.

Visits to Edgardo were few and far between since they could only occur when the family was invited by the Church. Each time they went the time spent together became increasingly colder until they never saw him again. Edgardo spent much time in the presence of Pope Pius IX, and finally became a priest. Edgardo's eagerness to be a Catholic may be compared to cases of the Stockholm Syndrome where the kidnapped person allies himself to his captors and even works with them. One only needs to recollect the kidnapping of Pattie Hearst, the millionaire's daughter in the USA, who joined in with her kidnappers and went on bank heists with them. Edgardo left Italy after some years because he was afraid that his parents would try to get him back. He lived in Belgium and Switzerland, and practiced as a priest until he died in 1940 at the age of 88.

The Edgardo affair blew up into an international incident. There were those who agreed with what the Catholic Church had done and those that were followers of the Enlightenment who felt that it was insensitive and wrong to force a religion upon anyone. Sir Moses Montefiore was a Jew from Livorno, Italy who was residing in England and had been knighted by the Queen. He had been successful in saving the life of a Jew from

Damascus who was about to be put to death for having allegedly killed a Christian boy for the purpose of requiring his blood in order to make matzo for Passover. Therefore Sir Moses was called in by the Jews of Bologna to help with the Mortara affair, but he was unsuccessful against the intransigence of the Pope.

Throughout history Jews have been considered to be the killers of Christ by the Catholic Church. Matters changed in the last 40 years when Pope John XXIII and Pope John Paul II removed the blame of the crucifixion of Christ from the Jews. John Paul II was a friend of the Jews, but when he beatified Pope Pius IX of the Edgardo Mortara affair the Jews were most unhappy with him for doing so. Also, in 2011 Pope Benedict XVI condemned Nazi ideology and said that he wished to create a greater friendship between Catholics and the Jews. However, Jews lost faith in his promises when he rescinded the excommunication of Richard Williamson, a Holocaust denier, from the Catholic Church. They considered it a "slap in the face". Incidentally Stephen Spielberg made a film about Edgardo Montara, but the Catholic Church would not allow him to distribute it. It still remains unseen by the general public.

So how could we put an end to anti-Semitism? In 1860 Theodor Herzl was born in Pest, which later became a part of Budapest in Hungary. Later in his life he moved to Vienna, still within the Austro-Hungarian Empire. He was a secular Jew, like his parents but unlike his grandparents who were religious Jews. He was a journalist and playwright, and was much enamored with the German culture. He soon resigned from the German cultural society to which he belonged when he recognized the anti-Semitism amongst his fellow members. He then tried to publish some articles about existent anti-Semitism in the papers for which he worked as a journalist, but the editor refused to accept them for publication so he wrote a book about the subject called "Der Judenstaat" – the State of the Jews. In the book he suggested that anti-Semitism cannot be eradicated and anti-Semites would never change their minds. The only hope for the Jews was to have their own land where they can live freely and peacefully. He said that Jews naturally drifted to the lands where there was no persecution, but in a short time persecution occurred there too. His plans were accepted and discussed by Jews all over the civilized world, although he did get some opposition from groups of Orthodox Jews who thought this matter was in the hands of God alone. Herzl maintained that the world would be enriched by their ideas and teachings, wealth and intellectual development. Humanity would benefit from this new Jewish land.

He said that he first thought about Zionism when he read about the Dreyfus Trial in France. Dreyfus was a Jewish officer in the French army. He had been accused of passing on military secrets to the Germans, and found guilty. He was sentenced to life imprisonment on Devil's Island, off the coast of French Guiana, South America. At the trial and in the press, anti-Semitism was rife. Many years later at a re-trial Dreyfus was found to be innocent, and another officer turned out to be the guilty one. Some have said that Herzl originally felt that Dreyfus was guilty, and only after the later trial did he realize his innocence, like everybody else. The trial demonstrated blatant anti-Semitism at work. They say that another cause for Herzl's turning to Zionism was the rabid anti-Semitism of Karl Lueger of Vienna who was Adolph Hitler's hero.

In order to set about achieving his goal of a Jewish state Herzl started off by meeting with the German Kaiser. He then went to visit the Grand Vizier, followed by the Sultan of the Ottoman Empire, in whose Empire Palestine existed. He offered financial retribution to help the Turks offset their large debts in exchange for a Jewish state within the Ottoman Empire. Nothing came of that, but he did receive a medal of honor from the Sultan. He went to London, where he met members of the British cabinet and spoke to huge crowds. The British made a suggestion of Uganda as a land for the Jews. This idea was discussed for a while, but it was soon forgotten. Uganda, unlike Jerusalem, had not existed in the hearts and the lives of the Jews for the last two millennia. There was no deep inner feeling for Uganda. Ever since the expulsion from the Holy Land the Jews have been praying "Next year in Jerusalem".

Zionism was growing and spreading amongst the Jews all over the world. The 1st Zionist Conference which was presided over by Herzl was held in Basel in 1897, and it was attended by Jews from many different countries from all over the world. Herzl then went to visit Jerusalem and spoke to the Jews there. He tried to get the Pope interested in a home for the Jews but he was told that as long as the Jews deny Christ there will be no help coming from the Catholic Church.

The rest is history. In 1948 Israel came into existence. After 6 million

Jews had been massacred Zionism became the main thrust of the Jewish people, which won them a land. The United Nations voted in favor of dividing up Palestine into a home for the Jews and one for the Arabs. Herzl's labors did not go unanswered. Unfortunately, he did not live to see Israel as a national home for the Jews because he died in 1904 at the age of 44. After Israel became a Jewish homeland in 1948 Herzl's body was moved to Jerusalem.

However, the specter of anti-Semitism did not die with the birth of Israel. On a number of occasions the surrounding Arab countries have attacked the infant state, each time Israel has defeated them and grown a little larger. Jews have been accused by their enemies that they are treating the Palestinians in a similar manner in which they were treated by the Fascists. Of course, such a comparison is ludicrous. There is no slaughtering of masses of people or concentration camps. In fact, there are camps set up by neighboring Arab states where Palestinian have been living for seventy years at the expense of the United Nations. They have not been made citizens in the lands in which they reside. Palestinians living in Israel are treated more democratically than those living in neighboring Arab lands. On at least three occasions the Israelis offered the Palestinians the West Bank and Gaza, and they would not accept it. There have been constant intifadas and terrorism which necessitated Israel to maintain order. It appears as though the Arabs will not be happy until the last Jew leaves the Middle East. This has been reiterated by their leaders on a number of occasions. Hezbollah and Hamas, armed by Iran and Syria constantly attack Israeli territory with missiles and other weapons. However, at this time the Jews seem to have more friends among the Arabs, since the common enemy seems to be Iran, and some Arab states feel that they can probably receive more protection from being friendly with Israel than being its enemy. The United Arab Emirates and Bahrain have joined Egypt and Jordan in being at peace and trading with Israel.

There are some Jews, both in the United States and Israel who support and empathize with the Palestinians in their plight and blame Israel for it. Is this Jewish anti-Semitism? It is true that the children of yesterday's Zionists are not as nationalistic as their parents were in the past. Their parents suffered and died in the Holocaust and in the Israeli-Arab wars.

They had good reason to be avid Zionists whereas their children have led much easier lives.

It has been said the Jews do not complain enough about their suffering from anti-Semitic acts and words. They are so inured from millennia of attacks of hatred and so ashamed that they don't talk about it. Why don't they march, complain, call for understanding? Women might not have received the vote in the US if not for their marching and complaining. Black People in the US claiming that "Black Lives Matter" have gained White marchers at their demonstrations and empathy from numerous other sources. If Jews emulated the women marchers and the Black Lives Matter campaigns perhaps people will begin to notice and react.

As Amos Oz, a famous Israeli author, once said – There was a time when the Jew-baiters of Europe stated "We don't want you in our country. Go to Palestine where you belong!" They now say "Get out of Israel. You have no right to be living on Palestinian soil!" The anti-Semites have found no place for the Wandering Jew.